Standards in Practice Grades 6–8

Standards in Practice Grades 6–8

Jeffrey D. Wilhelm

National Council of Teachers of English
1111 W. Kenyon Road, Urbana, Illinois
61801–1096

Manuscript Editor: Sheila A. Ryan
Production Editor: Peter Feely
Cover and Interior Design: R. Maul
Cover and Interior Photographs: Thompson-McClellan Photography

NCTE Stock Number: 46945-3050

It is the policy of NCTE in its journals and other publications to provide a forum for the open discussion of ideas concerning the content and the teaching of English and the language arts. Publicity accorded to any particular point of view does not imply endorsement by the Executive Committee, the Board of Directors, or the membership at large, except in announcements of policy, where such endorsement is clearly specified.

Although every attempt is made to ensure accuracy at the time of publication, NCTE cannot guarantee that published electronic mail addresses are current.

Library of Congress Cataloging-in-Publication Data

Wilhelm, Jeffrey D., 1959-
Standards in practice, grades 6-8 / Jeffrey D. Wilhelm.
p. cm.
Includes bibliographical references.
ISBN 0-8141-4694-5
1. Language arts—United States. 2. Language arts—Standards--United States. I. Title.
LB1576.W48766 1996
372.6'044-dc20 95-49758
CIP

FOREWORD

This book is one of four in the NCTE Standards in Practice series. The idea for this series grew out of requests from many teachers around the country who participated in the development of the NCTE/IRA standards and who asked if we could publish a book or a series of books that would illustrate what the standards might look like in actual classrooms at different grade levels.

This request was both inviting and challenging. Because one of the main goals of NCTE is to support classroom teachers, providing a series of books that would help define the standards seemed like the sort of thing we should do—and it is the type of thing, we like to think, we do quite well. At the same time, there were many challenges in developing these books. We wondered: Could we do it? What might these books look like? What standards would we use? How important would uniformity and consistency be among the books in the series?

The four authors and I spent time exploring these questions and it soon became evident that the development of this series was, perhaps, both simpler and even more important than we had originally thought. We decided that if we asked English language arts teachers who were doing interesting and challenging work in their classrooms to reflect in writing on their practices and to tell us their stories, the standards would be there, already at work in students' learning. After all, the English language arts standards did emerge from those practices that our membership and the IRA membership said they valued most. The standards do not stand above and apart from the practices of actual classroom teachers, or dictate to them—rather they represent what those teachers and the many others involved in English language arts education agree is the best and most productive current thinking about teaching and learning. We also decided that each book in the series did not have to follow the same generic format. What each book should do instead is tell its own story and use the format that best fits and supports the story or stories being told.

All of us agreed that we wanted the books in this series to be stories or rich illustrations of classroom practice. Stories, we thought, would allow the writers to capture the rich and complex activities of teaching and learning and, in addition, would illustrate the interconnectedness of the English language arts and of the standards themselves. We also wanted our readers to see how teachers create contexts as well as learning experiences. We thought it was important for the readers to experience both the struggles *and* the successes teachers and students encounter. And we hoped that the stories would make explicit the importance of the teacher as researcher: We believe the standards are dynamic in nature and will change and improve only if teachers actively and deliberately interrogate their own practice—learning and growing from their professional and classroom experiences.

In these four books we meet caring teachers who meet all our most challenging criteria for teaching and learning. They are women and men who think deeply about the quality of life and intellectual growth they provide for their students. Some of the teachers we meet in the series are new to the profession and are trying out ideas for the first time. Others have been teaching for many years but, as always, are reflecting on and questioning some of their practices, and in their stories we see them making changes. All of them, whether they are teaching five-year-olds or eighteen-year-olds, whether they themselves have been teaching for five or for eighteen or more years, put students' learning at the center of their curricula and engage their students in challenging, authentic experiences. By presenting an array of classroom portraits, these volumes clearly show that standards are always present in good practice and that there is no one way for the standards to be realized.

I want to commend the teachers and students who are featured in this series and the writers who told their stories. They have opened their classrooms to us and let us look in, and, in so doing, they have enriched our understandings of what matters most in the English language arts.

—Karen Smith
Associate Executive Director
National Council of Teachers of English

Contents

NCTE/IRA Standards for the English Language Arts

The vision guiding these standards is that all students must have the opportunities and resources to develop the language skills they need to pursue life's goals and to participate fully as informed, productive members of society. These standards assume that literacy growth begins before children enter school as they experience and experiment with literacy activities—reading and writing, and associating spoken words with their graphic representations. Recognizing this fact, these standards encourage the development of curriculum and instruction that makes productive use of the emerging literacy abilities that children bring to school. Furthermore, the standards provide ample room for the innovation and creativity essential to teaching and learning. They are not prescriptions for particular curriculum or instruction.

Although we present these standards as a list, we want to emphasize that they are not distinct and separable; they are, in fact, interrelated and should be considered as a whole.

1. Students read a wide range of print and nonprint texts to build an understanding of texts, of themselves, and of the cultures of the United States and the world; to acquire new information; to respond to the needs and demands of society and the workplace; and for personal fulfillment. Among these texts are fiction and nonfiction, classic and contemporary works.

2. Students read a wide range of literature from many periods in many genres to build an understanding of the many dimensions (e.g., philosophical, ethical, aesthetic) of human experience.

3. Students apply a wide range of strategies to comprehend, interpret, evaluate, and appreciate texts. They draw on their prior experience, their interactions with other readers and writers, their knowledge of word meaning and other texts, their word identification strategies, and their understanding of textual features (e.g., sound-letter correspondence, sentence structure, context, graphics).

4. Students adjust their use of spoken, written, and visual language (e.g., conventions, style, vocabulary) to communicate effectively with a variety of audiences and for different purposes.

5. Students employ a wide range of strategies as they write and use different writing process elements appropriately to communicate with different audiences for a variety of purposes.

6. Students apply knowledge of language structure, language conventions (e.g., spelling and punctuation), media techniques, figurative language, and genre to create, critique, and discuss print and nonprint texts.

7. Students conduct research on issues and interests by generating ideas and questions, and by posing problems. They gather, evaluate, and synthesize data from a variety of sources (e.g., print and nonprint texts, artifacts, people) to communicate their discoveries in ways that suit their purpose and audience.

8. Students use a variety of technological and informational resources (e.g., libraries, databases, computer networks, video) to gather and synthesize information and to create and communicate knowledge.

9. Students develop an understanding of and respect for diversity in language use, patterns, and dialects across cultures, ethnic groups, geographic regions, and social roles.

10. Students whose first language is not English make use of their first language to develop competency in the English language arts and to develop understanding of content across the curriculum.

11. Students participate as knowledgeable, reflective, creative, and critical members of a variety of literacy communities.

12. Students use spoken, written, and visual language to accomplish their own purposes (e.g., for learning, enjoyment, persuasion, and the exchange of information).

Acknowledgments

There are many people to thank when one engages in such a short and intense writing experience as this one turned out to be. My thanks to Karen Smith of NCTE and to my readers/peer editors, who worked under tremendous constraints to get this project done on time: Yvonne Siu-Runyan, Diane Orchard, and Elizabeth Close.

Most of all, I wish to thank those colleagues and team-teaching partners who have made my teaching such an exciting adventure over the past thirteen years. I wish to thank my teammates Paul Friedemann and Judy Bovee. Their collaboration, careful thought, planning, support, and insight over the years we worked together allowed many exciting things to happen for our students. Thank you to Brian Ambrosius for his professional guidance and friendship.

I also would like to thank those university contacts who supported the implementation of many of the projects described in this book: Brian Edmiston, Patricia Enciso, Richard Lehrer, and Julie Erickson of the University of Wisconsin-Madison; David Schaafsma of Columbia University Teachers College; and Michael W. Smith of Rutgers University.

Dedication

I dedicate this book
to my most persistent teachers:
my students;
my wife, Peggy Jo;
my children, Fiona and Jasmine;
and my mentor, Michael W. Smith.

Chapter One

National Standards, Community Conversations

To teach. That was what Judy (who represents a real teacher) had always wanted to do.

To be a teacher. It seemed to her to be a calling, one of those pursuits in this world most worth the doing. A vocation, an act of faith in the future, the job of jobs. The only other career she had even briefly considered was medicine.

When people asked her what she did, she proudly told them, "I'm a teacher," and the act of teaching and her identity, the doing and the being, were like synonymous and synchronous chambers of her innermost heart.

Community was an important thing to Judy. She liked the idea that she taught in the town where she had lived for the past seventeen years, that she had helped a generation of students on their journey through school and into the joy and problems, the art and business of living. She liked, too, to be a part of a community of teachers, a community of learners, a community of teachers *as* learners. She liked being a member of what she considered to be a most necessary profession.

When she was in the Peace Corps in Jamaica, she remembered sitting on top of a hill towards evening. The sky was splashed with brilliant red streaks across a darkening cobalt blue. She was with an old man who had been the teacher for the village below. He picked up his cane and swept it across the valley. "I have taught everyone in this village. I have educated the generations," he told her, and then fell silent again. That had really impressed Judy. Here was a man whose life was intertwined with every life in his community. He had made a commitment to the humanity of this place and he could watch the commitment unfold and be fulfilled. What satisfaction that must be! Though not as old and bent as her Jamaican friend, she was beginning to feel some of his satisfaction.

Seventeen years. Judy could hardly believe that she had been teaching the language arts for seventeen years. And every year brought new challenges. When she had started she was overwhelmed by what she felt to be the awesome responsibility and complexity of teaching. It was as exciting, exhilarating, and exhausting a profession as one could imagine. It was interesting to her that at the outset of her career she had conceived of her responsibility primarily as dispensing information, and she was terrified by how little she knew. Now she felt her responsibility was to facilitate and guide student learning, helping students to construct meaning. Part of that responsibility was to articulate goals—or standards—to identify what students should know and be able to do with what they know.

Judy taught in a growing suburban district near a large midwestern city. The population of the school was steadily growing, more and more racially diverse families were moving to the area, and the community work force was becoming more engaged in the light industries and services as the neighboring farms were gobbled up by housing developments. And changes, as always, bring challenges.

About seven years ago the junior high where Judy taught began the transition to becoming a middle school. At that time, the school divided into houses and teams of teachers. The teams were made up of five or six teachers representing different content areas. There was staff development and an invitation to transform the curriculum "delivery" (a term Judy disliked) into student-centered themes. Important skills and content could be embedded in these integrated units, and there was an understanding that teaching teams would have some freedom to transform the content of their courses as they designed these units.

After seven years, the different teams were at different points on their journey towards a more student-centered and integrated curriculum. Some teams had designed and implemented units integrating all of the subject areas. Other teams, like Judy's, worked in pairs or triads on various units that integrated content and skills primarily from two or three subject areas. Still other teams continued to teach their individual classes independently, according to the junior high model, or tried to teach units with similar themes during the same time of year without actually team teaching or integrating assignments. Everybody, including Judy and her teammates, was struggling to move in small ways towards better middle school teaching.

The teams taught all of the students assigned to their particular house. Judy's team met daily, worked to integrate instruction, and tried hard to work together to help all of the students in their "school within a school." This was their special challenge, because Judy's house served all of the students at that grade level who were labeled EEN, or as having exceptional educational needs. This year she would have a total of 130 students, and about fifteen were labeled LD (learning disabled), four were labeled as ED (emotionally disturbed), and several were also labeled as ESL (English as a Second Language). Most of these ESL students were Chicano or Hmong, although there were small but growing populations of Portuguese and Polish immigrants as well. All of these ESL students were judged as proficient enough in their English language ability to benefit from mainstreaming.

While conversing one night on the Internet's xtar discussion group on teacher research, Judy had complained that her EEN students' only real problem was that they were "severely *labeled*" and that "they didn't learn in the ways schools privilege learning. They have talents and strengths and intelligences, but they are not recognized or rewarded by the ways we typically do things in school."

Judy smiled to herself as she thought about Rick, who ran around the hallways making motor noises. Rick's father owned a stock car, and Rick would spend his weekends at the track. He was labeled LD and really struggled in school. He was a tremendously friendly kid with a quick smile. But he could not, would not, absolutely refused to read—despite all of Judy's best efforts.

Students apply a wide range of strategies to comprehend, interpret, evaluate, and appreciate texts. They draw on their prior experience, their interactions with other readers and writers, their knowledge of word meaning and other texts, their word identification strategies, and their understanding of textual features (e.g., sound-letter correspondence, sentence structure, context, graphics).

In spite of Rick's friendly brand of recalcitrance, Judy was frustrated and had once or twice snapped at him. She blamed his problems on his learning disability and a lack of motivation. One rainy day, she could not start her car. Who emerged from the building, without a coat, fresh from detention? Who but Rick. "Release the hood," he told her and she obeyed. "Got any WD-40?" She did. He sprayed it on the spark plugs and the wires leading to them. "Turn it over." She did and the engine roared to life. Sopping wet, he leaned in her open window. "The viscosity of the oil draws out the water and seals the wires so you can get your spark." And with a wave he was off, before Judy could offer him a ride. She wondered who was LD now. Later in the school year, she successfully encouraged Rick to read by asking him to research and create his own illustrated auto manual for people who knew nothing about cars.

One of Judy's guiding principles as a teacher was to "make sure that kids know their education is about *them*." She thought back again to last year and one of her Hmong students named Tongo, who had arrived in this country from Thailand only a few months earlier. Though he struggled mightily through the early part of the year, she had involved him by encouraging him to illustrate, dramatize, and then write stories about what it was like in Laos, in the camps of Thailand, and what it was now like to be a newly arrived immigrant. In this way he was able to teach his classmates and help them to know him. Later in the year he was the point man for his group's cultural journalism project about Laos. He brought in his family for interviews and provided many cultural artifacts that had helped his group in their study. He had become a part of the class and had used his past to find a place in the present.

Students develop an understanding of and respect for diversity in language use, patterns, and dialects across cultures, ethnic groups, geographic regions, and social roles.

Judy wanted to help all of her students learn and build from their strengths—to see themselves as meaning makers, readers, and writers. She wanted to help them use language with fluency and control to gain knowledge, create ideas, and solve problems. She saw the role of the teacher as an enabler, a landscape architect creating climates of opportunity, choice, and possibility where students could exercise agency and ownership as they learned.

The diverse needs of her students, the changes in her school and community, the demands of working as a team, all of these challenges made Judy consider the question: What is literacy? For her, it used to be the ability to read and write well enough to succeed in school and at work. She thought about this quite often. For example, the other day she was at a fast food restaurant and was being served by a former student when the electricity went out. "Oh no," he said, turning a horrified eye at the blinking cash register, "now I'll have to do it the *old fashioned* way." After rummaging in a drawer for a moment, he pulled out a calculator. It was an amusing incident, but it made her think again about the kind of world that students live and will work in.

Now, Judy was coming to think of literacy as the ability to comprehend, interpret, critique, and construct meanings with a variety of symbols and tools. In this quickly changing world, students needed the ability to traffic in signs and meanings, whether it be with technology or with a pencil and a book. To help serve her evolving definition, she and her social studies partner Peter had begun using a lot of student-centered and student-designed learning projects that involved drama, art, computers, hypermedia, and video. What was the goal? She wanted her students to become informed and critical citizens, trafficking in culturally relevant systems of signs and meanings, who worked for democracy. But what did it mean to be a democratic citizen anyway? For Judy, a democratic citizen was an individual who could pursue her own meanings and happiness, do useful and fulfilling work, exercise informed choices, work for justice and the good of the community.

As she thought about the approaching school year, there was yet another challenge and consideration, and it was lying on the middle of her desk: the national standards. How should she think about them? How should they inform her own work?

Judy was actually pretty excited about receiving the standards. She regarded her whole career as a conversation, a grand dialogue with students, parents, colleagues, authors, and the profession itself about how to best educate our children. Judy was a member of both the National Council of Teachers of English and the International Reading Association, the two groups that had collaborated to create the standards document. It was important to her that teachers like herself, from all levels, had been an integral part of drafting the document.

Now that the document lay on her desk, it seemed like another opportunity to dialogue with her profession. The standards were concerned with professional knowledge and helped to explore a philosophical basis for teacher decision making. They were also concerned with what students should be able to know and do and how teachers could help make this possible. The standards therefore reflected much of the best of what was currently thought and known in language arts education. They were a conversation about the challenge of the future, about the needs of students in that future, about what preparation students needed for lifelong literacy. The standards were a dialogue about doing her job well, about helping her students to become independent learners and thinkers. That was a conversation in which Judy wanted to take part.

Judy had originally approached the standards with some apprehensions. In her experience, there was often a tension between progressive child-centeredness and the setting of higher standards. She wanted to enable and help *all* of her students, not sort them into categories, and she sometimes had a feeling that higher standards required a lot of kids to fail. Sorting the wheat from the chaff and all that. Judy felt that her job, no matter what new challenges emerged, remained essentially the same: to come to know and to teach *all* of the real kids who came through her door—no matter what their past or their label.

She wanted to raise the ante for all of her students. What she wanted was greater success for more students measured against higher standards for knowing and doing.

With apologies to Bobby McFerrin, one of Judy's favorite epigrams was "Be Happy, Not Satisfied." When she finished a lesson or a school year she wanted to celebrate the success of the students and the hard, worthwhile, and noble work she had done; but she always tried to keep in mind that she and her students could do better.

Students use a variety of technological and informational resources (e.g., libraries, databases, computer networks, video) to gather and synthesize information and to create and communicate knowledge.

Students conduct research on issues and interests by generating ideas and questions, and by posing problems. They gather, evaluate, and synthesize data from a variety of sources (e.g., print and nonprint texts, artifacts, people) to communicate their discoveries in ways that suit their purpose and audience.

Judy had read through the standards, looking for challenges to her thinking. Did she agree with the standards? Did they reflect her values? Could they help her teach better? Did they help her to think about ways to invite students into the classroom as learners; to know and understand them; to offer them a repertoire of ways to know, understand, and grow themselves; to connect themselves to the world and find a place in it?

Her first reading of the standards document had made her think about how to include more of the kids' concerns and experiences in her teaching, how to blend speaking, listening, and media literacy into her reading and writing assignments, how to include more about language and about cultural diversity. These were not new issues for Judy, but the standards helped her to view them yet again, and with a new lens.

She wanted to consciously run her class with respect for her kids and their backgrounds. She wanted to be direct and kind with them, to listen attentively and take them seriously. That meant attending to their individual needs and interests *and* guiding them clearly towards becoming more powerful and self-actualized people. It was a high-wire act balanced between what they knew, what they wanted to know, and what they needed to know. So always there was the unceasing question hovering in the air: What did they need to know and be able to do?

Judy felt that almost everything she knew about teaching was contingent, situational, and categorically tentative. Teaching, to her, was the struggle to remain open to meeting new challenges and opportunities. She didn't look to the standards to solve that condition, but to increase the openness by encouraging teachers to think once again, as a community, about what to do and how to do it better.

Although it was a few days before the inservices and the beginning of the school year, Judy and several other teachers were already at work in their classrooms. Later that day, two of her colleagues in the language arts department congregated in her room. Rob and Diane both had their copies of the national standards and wanted to talk about them.

Rob taught down the corridor from Judy, and she had nicknamed him "John Dewey Junior." His teaching always took astonishing directions. This past year, while reading C. S. Lewis's *The Voyage of the Dawn Treader*, his students had become interested in researching island habitats and other isolated ecosystems. When they were done, a giant papier-mâché rainforest was growing out of his classroom and into the hallway. And money had been raised through various initiatives to buy two acres of rainforest in Central America for perpetual preservation.

Diane was wearing a T-shirt that announced, "I know it can't be true because I heard it in the teachers' lounge." She taught on the second floor and was a bit more traditional than Judy or Rob. She still used the anthology (Judy used it as a resource, and Rob didn't use it at all) and was fairly careful to try and address not only the spirit but also the letter of the department's published curriculum, which antedated the school's transition to middle school status. But she wasn't afraid to adapt instruction or use the textbook in creative ways. She had been through the National Writing Project and did great work with her student writers, publishing lots of their work in her role as editor of the school literary magazine. She was a doer and organized schoolwide book swaps, read-ins, a homeroom-sustained silent reading program, and a summer reading initiative. Judy regarded both of her colleagues and friends, different as they were, as excellent teachers and as intelligent innovators.

Last year, the three had written and shared metaphors for teaching. All three had come up with journey metaphors, but with very different roles for themselves. Rob's role on the journey was to "help them get to the library, the zoo, the woodshop or a pond, or wherever they want to go and set them loose. See what they find." Judy's role was to act as an "adventure guide" on a "somewhat planned safari," to shape the environment, guide the learners, help set up and engage them in challenging activities that they had a voice in creating. Diane was a "tour guide leading the class" through the itinerary laid out for the journey, "pointing out items of importance" and "encouraging occasional side trips."

Rob had just picked up his copy of the standards and his dander was up. "Here we go again!" he complained. "It looks like some more top-down spoon-feeding from those who live in ivory towers! Teaching once again reduced to a set of recipes. Let the oatmeal cooking begin!"

"Whoa, Rob, slow down there," Judy teased. "Let me quote one of your favorite sayings: 'We aren't successful unless our students are successful.' I've read through this and it's *not* a national curriculum like they have in Japan and other places. This is a set of shared professional understandings about what kids should be able to know and do. As a profession, we need to clearly define what those things are so that we can ask how to teach them and how we'll know when students have achieved them. As professionals, we need to know what we are trying to accomplish, how to do it, and how to know we've done it."

Diane broke in, "If we don't have special expertise, if any Joe on the street can teach, then we're not a profession. Besides, Rob," she continued, "almost all of your work with students involves getting them to build their own critical standards about their own work and about what's going on or could go on in the world. And you do that through conversation and comparison. If it's important for students, it's certainly important for teachers too."

Rob laughed. "You tag-teamers have really put it to me! Still," he mused, "there's something I don't like about it. Curriculum, to me, is something you negotiate and create with students, not something that can be planned or set out ahead of time."

"Rob, listen up! Clean the potatoes out of your ears! This is *not* a national curriculum."

"Oh, come on, Judy. Should standards be first, or should they emerge from good classroom practice? Should they come from what a bureaucrat values or what real teachers in real classrooms have come to value . . . ?"

Judy interrupted him, "Rob, these standards *did* emerge from good teaching practices . . ."

But Rob plowed on, "You know as well as I do that standards will be set and then the bureaucrats will have to assess whether kids meet the standards. And *that* is going to change what and how we teach. Curriculum will become a race course to run students around, as its Latin root word suggests, instead of a path of discovery like it should be. Standards are going to impact on curriculum. You know they will!"

"Of course. But the standards are only being stated. It's up to us, individual teachers in individual schools, to enact the standards. If we don't, nothing will change for the kids. So it's up to us to think about the standards and decide how they will inform our teaching. It seems to me that the standards should provide a broad framework for purposeful planning. It's kind of like providing a notion of a kitchen and the kinds of things you should be able to do in one, but still leaving it up to us to choose recipes and serve meals. Standards should create possibilities, not preclude them."

"I don't like that kitchen metaphor, Jude," Diane complained. "I know I'm traditional, but I want to keep my classroom a classroom."

"Instead of what?" Rob prodded. "Instead of a learning environment? Instead of a slice of life?"

Diane turned to him. "You know, I think I do well for my kids—they like me and my class—they learn. That doesn't mean that I'm not willing to consider making some changes, but I want to be careful about fixing what's not broke."

"There are a lot of ways to teach well," Judy reminded her. "If we all came from the same mold, that would make the kids' education less rich—but still, the key to making education better is a broad kind of shared vision so that we can make intelligent changes and educate each other and the public with some awareness."

"What *does* bug me about the standards," Diane said, "is that they're too interpretive, not factual enough—maybe even too politically correct or something—not explicit enough about things like grammar and the literary canon . . ."

"The specifics are being left up to us. That's part of the respect the standards grant us," Judy jumped in. Diane was left shaking her head.

"Geez," said Rob, "I had the opposite reaction, that the standards were too mainstream."

"Let me tell you something you *are* really going to like about the standards," Diane said to Rob, "once you've *really* read them! They emphasize that all students can learn. The standards ask us to value children's backgrounds and individuality. To take them, their language, what they say and how they learn, all with the utmost seriousness . . ."

"Like all of my teaching heroes, Vivian Paley, Maxine Greene, Gloria Ladson-Billings, my namesake John Dewey," Rob joked.

"Right," Diane continued, "and the standards are for everybody—for every single student. They are a vision of what is possible for every single child, and a vision of what they will be enabled to know and do as they live their lives."

"OK," Rob relented, "but these things are always an implicit slam on teachers, suggesting that we could do our jobs better and implying an agenda of how we could do so."

"This is Big Picture stuff, Rob," said Judy. "We can always do our jobs better. You embody that desire as much as anybody. Regarding the standards, it's up to us to test and interrogate them. They're meant to help us ask questions—and better questions lead to better practice and better results. We are the ones who will accept, reject, figure out, and deliver the details.

"And, Rob, this thing has been written with a lot of respect for teachers, students, and the acts of teaching and learning. It recognizes up front that teachers are being successful and that kids are learning more than ever before. The document asks me to consider and be open to alternatives and to test my professional conclusions instead of just listening to myself and looking in the mirror all the time. Hiding in my classroom would certainly be easier and less controversial, but ultimately it would be a lot less satisfying than engaging in conversation. People don't fight change, Rob; they fight the price they think change is going to make them pay. What price do *you* think that's going to be?"

Rob was silent a moment. "I'm not sure, but I want to be careful. The price could be big. We could lose some of our autonomy that helps us meet kids' needs . . . or definitions of good teaching could get set in concrete . . . become reified instead of creative, spontaneous, and open. Listen to this!" Rob said as he eagerly flipped through a copy of Frank Smith's *Insult to Intelligence*. "Let's see, page eighteen. Here it is. 'We underrate our brains and our intelligence. Formal education has become such a complicated, self-conscious and over-regulated activity that learning is widely regarded as something difficult that the brain would rather not do. . . . But reluctance to learn cannot be attributed to the brain. Learning is the brain's primary function, its constant concern, and we become restless and frustrated if there is no learning to be done. We are all capable of huge and unsuspected learning accomplishments without effort.' " Rob closed the book. "There. I believe that. That's why I don't want standards to lead to some more formalized, overdefined curriculum or method of teaching. It will just get in the way."

Judy agreed. "You should keep being careful, but be open too. A lot of what the standards do is articulate general principles: learning is a process; we have to start with student backgrounds, needs, and interests; learning is best when students *do* the things to be learned, when they actively construct their own meanings . . . I think I'm already meeting most of these standards, but I'm asking how to do it better, and other standards are really making me think hard. As I've been thinking about this coming school year, the standards have helped me to ask a lot of questions."

"What kinds of questions?" Rob and Diane asked almost simultaneously.

Judy picked up a list from her desk and the three laughed. She was famous for her lists and schedules and notes to herself. A study hall student last year had called her "Ms. List-Maker the Attendance Taker."

"All right," Judy said, "this is what I've got: What are worthwhile and personally urgent tasks that involve the language arts? How can I engage student interests *and* develop understanding and strategies? How can I move more towards a student-designed learning environment where kids ask their own questions, find information, organize it, analyze it, add to it, represent what they've found out in a variety of ways, revise it, and share it? How can I provide for student choice yet still have curriculum that is a coherent whole? How can I be more sensitive to and accommodate diversity in student backgrounds, learning styles, needs, and interests? How can I focus more on the importance of culture? How can I approach content and help students to connect to it? What can the group do: how can they teach and support each other? In short, how can I make what we do together an intensely human pursuit of making meaning with the language arts?"

"Reading through the standards stimulated those questions?" Diane asked.

Judy nodded as Rob said, "What I like about that list, Jude, is that it asks, 'What are the language arts for?' And like all the other subjects, language arts aren't an end in themselves but a means to larger understandings and social actions. But those questions you asked are the kinds of questions we ask anyway, Judy."

"But, Rob, the standards are helping me to ask them again, in new and more specific ways. They provide a template to converse with, a reason and a means to think about pedagogy not only by myself, but with others. These standards should be part of an evolving, generative process, a part of a conversation about what matters and how to bring that about."

"What about parents?" Rob retorted. "They've all been to school, so they all think they know about schooling. What if things get too different from their idea of school? And then there's the issue of time and support. How are we going to enact more changes when we are already so overworked and have so many students?"

"The standards," Diane began, "aren't going to be a panacea, but they should work as a tool for change. They provide a kind of justification for what we do. And it will become apparent if schools and teachers can't address the spirit of the standards because of how little time and resources they have. It will encourage policy makers to consider what makes up an adequate opportunity to learn. It's a chance for us to educate parents too, since these standards are about professional knowledge and who we are as professionals. This is a chance," Diane concluded, "to professionally redefine ourselves for ourselves, for our students, and for the public. If we're not doing some of that, then we're not growing and changing and educating *ourselves* in the way that we are asking the kids to do for *themselves*. I don't think the standards are prescriptive–there are more things that would bug me about them if they were. I think they are very forward-looking, asking us to look ahead to what is possible for our students. Why are you laughing?"

Rob recovered from his chuckle. "I was just thinking that I would have expected you to be more skeptical of the standards."

"Maybe I was. I've said some things I don't like about the standards. I kept asking–but what kinds of materials should we use? Aren't there works of literature and rules of language everybody should know? Why aren't these specified? Then I thought maybe this isn't about *what* to teach but *how* to teach–so that students will own and be changed by what they do. Maybe it's not a question of what they should read now, but a question of what they should want and be able to read later in life. I still find this whole issue troublesome. But I've read the standards now and I'm ready to think and talk about them. I think it will push me in good ways, make me critical and wide-awake about justifying what I do and how I do it. By the way, why haven't *you* carefully read them, Rob?" Her tone was one she used with slightly recalcitrant students.

"Well," joked Rob, "I would have but Bounder ate them when I accidently laid them in the dog dish last night. But I've got a fresh copy and I'm off to read them right now!" And with a wave of his hand, he was gone.

"I guess it's time to start planning, try to think of ways to put some of these things I agree with into play," Judy told Diane as she sat down at her desk. "The hard thing will be to sequence things, to build some coherence through the year. To lay the groundwork to enable kids to reach for those higher level literacy standards. Because I want to increasingly provide kids with cultural tools for finding and expressing their own meanings."

"You bet. I'm looking forward to the next chapter of our conversation. And to hearing what Rob thinks when he's actually read the standards."

Judy laughed. "It kind of reminds me of whole language and lots of other ideas that I'm afraid could bite the dust without ever really being understood or tried. The standards should be a tool to help me take stock of where the field is, how I fit in it, where it's trying to go, how I can help or resist. It should be a powerful way to understand learning and teaching. I hope people aren't afraid to do that. Standards should encourage us to look hard at what we do, why we do it, encourage people to continue working on improving what they do, as well as to get out of the rut and be informed enough to try some new things. Yeah, pardner," she smiled, "there's a lot to think and talk about. Let's keep the conversation alive."

"If Rob were still here he'd quote Dewey: 'Democracy *is* conversation.'" And with a wave, Diane was off to her own room.

Judy sat alone at her desk and was revisited by that feeling, experienced so often earlier in her career, of the awesome responsibility of the teacher to touch and shape the future. What students know and are able to do, the choices they will be able to exercise, what they will be enabled to become depends in part on the opportunities they are given in school. Judy was gratified that the standards recognized that education happens where the rubber hits the road–where teachers and students and opportunities meet, with all the daily diversity and complexity that entails.

The important and difficult work of educating is pursued between teacher and student in whatever environment opportunity arises. So the success of the educational enterprise depends on what they do together, and only the teacher will be there to recognize and actualize the opportunity in the best way for those individual students. The task of the profession is to equip teachers to act and choose, not to prescribe.

For these reasons, articulating and considering standards seemed to Judy to be both a practical venture and an ethical imperative. All teaching, whether we are conscious of it or not, deals with the awesome choice of what knowledge, experiences, and abilities are most worthwhile and useful to our children. And then all teaching must consider the question: What are the best ways of helping each student to live through, own, and make use of what is so important to being human in our culture?

And there was so much Judy wanted for all of her kids. Certainly that they could communicate with others through reading, writing, speaking, and listening. But there was much more than that: that they could find, analyze, and

POINTS TO CONSIDER:

- Standards are *not* a national curriculum.
- Standards *are* an attempt to define what students should be able to know and do.
- The standards are informed by the latest theory and research regarding language arts education.
- Standards are field based; they build on past successes of teachers and students.
- Standards can be met through a variety of teaching styles and strategies.
- The standards project emphasizes that *all* students can learn and achieve at high levels if their background, needs, and interests are considered.
- Standards should be a source of professional conversation and critique about what to do and how to do it.
- Teachers are members of a professional community, and there are a variety of professional organizations available to support teacher growth.
- The literacy demands of the 21st century will require students to construct meaning with a variety of tools and texts.

critique information and be strengthened and invigorated to act on what they knew. She wanted them to recognize and go about solving problems. She wanted them to be able to interact and get things done in communities, to recognize and cherish values, accept responsibility, understand and appreciate the various forms of art and how they express and explore the truths of human experience. There was so much she wanted for them. How could she help them on their journeys?

This was the importance of standards to Judy. They informed her thinking and her choices. This was vitally important because what we choose to do in classrooms is what enables the choice and possibilities of students, empowering them in the most human impulse and endeavor of growing and becoming and taking their place in the human community.

Teaching was the most powerful act Judy could conceive of because it enabled the choices of others. In many ways, teaching was an act of faith, situated in a vision and hope for the future, rooted in an environment of care and concern for others. Teaching, and how she went about it, undoubtedly shaped the future. And standards were a clear and powerful way of focusing on what she did.

Resources

Literacy as Exploration and Meaning Making

Brown, R. (1991). *Schools of thought: How the politics of literacy shape thinking in the classroom.* San Francisco: Jossey-Bass.

Davidson, J., & Koppenhaver, D. (1993). *Adolescent literacy: What works and why* (2nd ed.). New York: Garland.

Gere, A., Fairbanks, C., Howes, A., Roop, L., & Schaafsma, D. (1992). *Language and reflection: An integrated approach to teaching English.* New York: Macmillan.

Moffett, J., & Wagner, B. J. (1983). *Student-centered language arts and reading, K–13: A handbook for teachers* (3rd ed.). Boston: Houghton-Mifflin.

Purves, A. (Ed.). (1972). *How porcupines make love: Notes on a response-centered curriculum.* Lapington, MA: Xerox College Publishers.

Purves, A., Rogers, T., & Soter, A. O. (1990). *How porcupines make love II: Teaching a response-centered literature curriculum.* White Plains, NY: Longman.

Wilhelm, J. (in press). *Developing readers: Teaching engaged and reflective reading with adolescents.* New York: Teachers College Press.

Willinsky, J. (1990). *The new literacy: Redefining reading and writing in the schools.* New York: Routledge.

Reflective Practice

Grimmett, P., & Erickson, G. (1988). *Reflection in teacher education.* New York: Teachers College Press.

Grossman, P. L. (1990). *The making of a teacher: Teacher knowledge and teacher education.* New York: Teachers College Press.

Handal, G., & Lauvas, P. (1987). *Promoting reflective teaching: Supervision in practice.* Milton Keynes (Buckinghamshire); Philadelphia: Open University Press.

Rose, M. (1989). *Lives on the boundary.* New York: Free Press.

Schon, D. (1983). *The reflective practitioner: How professionals think in action.* New York: Basic Books.

Schon, D. (1987). *Educating the reflective practitioner: Toward a new design for teaching and learning in the professions.* San Francisco: Jossey-Bass.

Schon, D. (Ed.) (1991). *The reflective turn: Case studies in and on educational practice.* New York: Teachers College Press.

Tabachnick, B. R., & Zeichner, K. M. (1991). *Issues and practices in inquiry-oriented teacher education.* New York: Falmer.

Professional Associations

National Council of Teachers of English
1111 West Kenyon Road
Urbana, IL 61801-1096

International Reading Association
Headquarters Office
800 Barksdale Road
P.O. Box 8139
Newark, DE 19714-8139

National Middle School Association
2600 Corporate Exchange Drive, Suite 370
Columbus, OH 43231-1672

Association for Supervision and Curriculum Development
1250 North Pitt Street
Alexandria, VA 22314-1403

National Writing Project
University of California
School of Education
1615 University Hall
Berkeley, CA 94720

State and local associations

Chapter Two

Getting to Know You

Setting the Stage

Judy worked on a teaching team of five core teachers: science, math, social studies, language arts, and a learning specialist. Her students also took different exploratories and electives each quarter. The team had the same schedule, and this year the team taught their classes during periods 1, 2, 5, 6, and 7 during a 9-period day. Because they had the same schedule, two teachers would sometimes combine their classes, which meant that they would see each student twice that day in a team-taught situation. Since they had two big blocks of team time, they could often divide up kids and time in different ways to suit the purposes of integrated units. Judy's and Peter's classrooms were separated by a room divider, so it was easy to combine classes when they wanted.

The team also had scheduled team-planning time during period 3. Usually they met as a whole team once or twice a week to deal with general concerns. The other three or four days a week Judy met with Matt, the learning specialist, and Peter, the social studies teacher, to work on integrated unit planning. In the first semester they tried to parallel and support each other's instruction. In the second semester they often combined classes for team teaching as they pursued integrated learning projects in social studies and the language arts. This might mean that kids were taught in a large group, but more often it meant that they could use various work stations and pursue opportunities in both classrooms, the library, the computer lab, or other areas.

They had been working on some of their integrated units for the past three years, so a lot of things were already in place for this year. For example, a reading-buddy program with the elementary schools was already organized, and this would be their third year working on their big hypermedia project about culture.

Students conduct research on issues and interests by generating ideas and questions, and by posing problems. They gather, evaluate, and synthesize data from a variety of sources (e.g., print and nonprint texts, artifacts, people) to communicate their discoveries in ways that suit their purpose and audience.

They had tried to be articulate about what big understandings they wanted their students to construct through the integrated projects. There were procedural understandings about how to learn, like questioning, finding and creating information, inferring, organizing information, and representing it. And there were declarative understandings, too, regarding knowledge about the nature of culture, the importance of citizenship, how texts communicate meaning, and things like that.

For example, when Judy, Peter, and Matt (the learning specialist) began to plan their cultural journalism project, they started with the big understanding that groups of people create culture to express their values and fulfill their needs. They then worked to set up a project that would provide a series of occasions for approaching and considering this big understanding in specific terms. The big understanding they wanted students to achieve focused their planning and the students' work throughout the project.

Now they were considering a new project about citizenship and civil rights for the fourth quarter. The social studies standards asked that students come to understand how people create and change power structures to address social problems. The big understanding the three of them had identified as a starting point for their unit was that, when social problems persist, individuals and groups can find ways to influence public opinion and policy. Now they were planning how to provide experiences that would help students engage with this understanding.

Throughout their various projects, they also worked hard to acknowledge and appreciate the cultural and linguistic diversity of America and of their students.

This year Judy, Peter, and Matt would be building on and improving past units for which a lot of support and materials were already in place. But they were going to try some new things too. They were going to exchange two or three assignments with a partner school, and they were considering including a service component with their planned year-end project on citizenship and civil rights.

For a lot of the big integrated projects that Judy undertook with Peter and Matt, students would have 135 minutes of time each day with a teacher through their social studies, language arts, and resource-study periods. That really helped. The students would have sustained periods of time, with support, to work on their projects. They had been asking for block scheduling for the past several years, which would be even better, but that hadn't been worked out yet.

Sometimes when people came into their classrooms and saw what was happening, they were very impressed. It didn't seem all that amazing to Judy, Peter, or Matt though, until they compared what they were doing this year with what they had been doing three years ago. And they would stress to their visitors that "things take time."

They agreed that teaming doubled or trebled their teaching power—but it took time, good will, energy, and the willingness to push through and build on mistakes.

What would their classrooms look like this year? In three more years, given time and attention? Only the future would tell.

On the evening before the first day of school, Judy sat on her front porch swing conversing with her friends and sipping sangría. They noticed that she was a bit jittery. "Yes," she admitted, "even after seventeen years I'm still nervous before the first day. I just can't wait to meet my students, start getting to know them, and just get going!"

The next day, Judy introduced herself to her classes and set a few first expectations: "We are here to help each other learn and to learn from each other. There are twenty-seven teachers in this room and twenty-seven learners. In order to work together, we have to respect and be kind to each other." This, she knew, was a tall order for hormone-geysering, identity-probing twelve-year-olds. Some already looked like adults, and others looked like, well . . . like children. They came from different backgrounds and many had personal or family problems. Quite a few were labeled. And their behavior? She tried to remember a quotation from Rousseau's *Emile* that went something like this: "At times your student will soar like an eagle among the clouds and you will think him a prodigy. At other times he will wallow on the ground and you will think him a fool. In both cases you are mistaken: he is a child and both learns and has much to learn." Judy smiled to herself and thought that Rousseau must have had some experience with middle schoolers.

Judy explained that students were expected to come to class ready to learn and to cooperate, and to pursue the learning goals that the class would agree upon. She then detailed what she had come to call The Rule of Taste, "that we will try to never do anything that is unfair, that could offend or hurt someone else in our community. And if we do, we will apologize and correct ourselves. We want our class to be a haven of fairness." These few introductory expectations having been set, Judy told her students that there were some particular kinds of reading, writing, and learning to pursue this year, but that basically "this class begins with you. I want you to help me co-construct what we will do, how we will do it, and how we will evaluate it. You have a lot of responsibility to take on, and we may as well start right now."

Students adjust their use of spoken, written, and visual language (e.g., conventions, style, vocabulary) to communicate effectively with a variety of audiences and for different purposes.

Students conduct research on issues and interests by generating ideas and questions, and by posing problems. They gather, evaluate, and synthesize data from a variety of sources (e.g., print and nonprint texts, artifacts, people) to communicate their discoveries in ways that suit their purpose and audience.

Students use spoken, written, and visual language to accomplish their own purposes (e.g., for learning, enjoyment, persuasion, and the exchange of information).

To that end the students wrote a short vignette of a most memorable learning experience. They then shared the vignettes in small groups and tried to see similarities and patterns across their stories. When the patterns were shared with the large group, the students were surprised at how many of their most memorable learning experiences occurred outside of school or in an extracurricular activity. Common themes that they saw across the experiences were that the learning situation was often unique and different, they actively did or made something, they worked closely with other people, the experience was fun, it was active and hands-on, and they shared what they did or created with other people. In many cases the experience included different ways of knowing or expressing oneself: music, carpentry, art, dramatic performance, games, or simulations. What they did or made served some sort of personal purpose or solved a problem.

Judy told the students that when each of her five classes had come up with their list of common themes about memorable learning, then the "house" would have a model of the kind of learning experiences they wanted to pursue in language arts class during this year. Judy promised to make a poster outlining what the different classes agreed on as a rubric–or an outline–of memorable learning. Posted in the classroom, it would serve as a guidepost to be referred to and revised throughout the year.

For homework that night, Judy asked her students to complete a survey of their reading habits and attitudes and to write responses to these two questions: (1) describe your earliest memory as a reader, and (2) discuss a few of the most memorable significant events in your personal history as a reader and writer.

The Personality Profile Unit

The next day the students again shared their responses and looked for patterns. They discussed why people read and write, in what circumstances reading and writing are the most useful, the most powerful, the most pleasurable. Judy told the class that their first project would be to compose personality profiles. This assignment would serve as a way of introducing and presenting themselves to the class. She thought the experience would fit the model of memorable learning that they had constructed yesterday in class.

The profile would include whatever was important for others to know about them. Judy would also like them to include the issues they had already been discussing: the story of themselves as readers, writers, and learners.

She worked hard over the first few days of school to include the students, their experiences, and interests as part of the class. She wanted to convince them that the class would be a conversation that included them.

Judy liked starting the school year with composing personality profiles, and she had done so for the past several years. Most people like to talk about themselves and their interests. The kids all had something to say and seemed to enjoy saying it.

Two years ago, Judy decided to make two changes in the assignment: first, she changed the project from students writing about classmates to writing about themselves. This change gave them more ownership. It helped them with writer's block because the writing was based more closely on their personal knowledge. It also eliminated those few problems of students writing unkind things about each other, not getting along, and disputing quotations. Students could still go through the whole process, including conducting interviews with significant people in their lives. Judy thought it was important to start the year off positively and to help students bring themselves to the classroom. So she thought this change had worked to those ends.

Second, she had the students transfer onto hypercards the profiles they had written. This not only helped them to learn the hypercard program for future use during the integrated language arts and social studies units, but seemed to be highly motivating to the students as they typed their text onto the fields, scanned in pictures, created graphics, and recorded favorite music to go along with the text.

Students use a variety of technological and informational resources (e.g., libraries, databases, computer networks, video) to gather and synthesize information and to create and communicate knowledge.

Judy also liked the project because she believed that teaching students meant getting to know them. She also believed, as did one of her teaching heroes, Vivian Paley, that we must take seriously everything students do and say. The project helped set a tone of respect and a precedent that students will learn from each other. The project also served to pursue some of Judy's major goals for the students: developing the attitude that they were readers, writers, and learners; understanding that reading and writing were unique and powerful ways of knowing; growing in their ability to make inferences, organize information, and read for meaning.

Every year, Judy made notes during and after her units, and she revisited these notes if she pursued the same unit again. As she looked at last year's notes regarding the profile project, her former self advised her present self to "provide more opportunities for project to be viewed, read, and discussed by people outside of class" and to provide "more time for revision." So as she began to block out her lesson plans and sign up for computer-room times, she kept this advice to herself in mind.

Students adjust their use of spoken, written, and visual language (e.g., conventions, style, vocabulary) to communicate effectively with a variety of audiences and for different purposes.

Reciprocal Reading

During the second week of school, Judy began by giving the students an anticipatory guide about tigers and tiger hunting. After the students' prior knowledge had been activated and their interest piqued with such true-false statements as "A tiger hunter must often use himself as bait," Judy began reading a professional profile about Jim Corbett, the world's most famous tiger hunter. As she read the profile aloud, she introduced a technique called "reciprocal reading," which she had adapted from the professional literature (Palinscar & Brown, 1984; Brown & Palinscar, 1989) and which she planned for students to use in various ways throughout the year.

ANTICIPATORY GUIDE
PROFILE- JIM CORBETT, THE TIGER HUNTER

1. Man is a natural prey of the tiger.	T	F
2. Through the first half of this century there was only one hunter good enough to stalk and kill the most ferocious man-eating tigers.	T	F
3. To be a truly great hunter, one must devote their life to the skills of tracking, baiting and shooting.	T	F
4. Even the greatest hunter will fail to get his prey up to half of the time, even when he has unlimited time and resources for the hunt.	T	F
5. Some individual tigers have killed and eaten nearly 500 people.	T	F
6. If a tiger kills an Indian, then his wife must be killed and burned on his funeral pyre.	T	F
7. The best tiger hunters hunt alone.	T	F
8. Tiger hunters may try to call the tigers to them rather than stalking them and catching them by surprise.	T	F
9. Many hunters develop a sixth sense warning them of danger.	T	F
10. A tiger hunter must often use himself as bait.	T	F
11. A tiger would rather attack a woman than a man.	T	F
12. The largest concentration of tigers is found in Africa.	T	F

Judy modeled the procedure with different students as they read and responded to the text together. She emphasized that in reciprocal reading the group using the technique was responsible for understanding and evaluating the text. She started off modeling the technique with students, working with them as pairs, though later in the year they would work in groups of four.

First, the reader read aloud and the other student, designated as the leader, helped with any difficulties. When the reader had read the agreed upon section (a paragraph, a page, etc.), the leader asked a question about the main content, which the two then worked together to answer.

Then roles were switched. When the reading of a designated section was complete, attempts were made to clarify misunderstandings or disagreements. The leader then summarized the section, and together they worked on the summary until they agreed that all main ideas had been covered.

Students participate as knowledgeable, reflective, creative, and critical members of a variety of literacy communities.

Students apply a wide range of strategies to comprehend, interpret, evaluate, and appreciate texts. They draw on their prior experience, their interactions with other readers and writers, their knowledge of word meaning and other texts, their word identification strategies, and their understanding of textual features (e.g., sound-letter correspondence, sentence structure, context, graphics).

The reader was asked to make a prediction before roles were again switched, and the process continued.

Though Judy encouraged the groups to occasionally engage in open discussions, the group members did repeat a structured process of reading, questioning, clarifying, summarizing, and predicting. The technique introduced the structured use of simple group discussion techniques for understanding and remembering text content. The strategies provided a basic heuristic, or model, of what readers do as they construct meaning. While using the technique, the pairs or small groups of students provided social support, modeling, and a sharing of their experiences and expertise.

One of Judy's special challenges as a teacher was how to challenge all of her students and to provide them with a vital community role to play in the classroom. Already she knew that students like Troy and Nicky were exceptionally creative and advanced. Then there were students like Kae, a Hmong girl newly arrived from Laos—obviously bright but struggling with her new language and cultural situation—and Mike, sharp as a tack but with a history of problems in school. And of course there were labeled students, like Tim and Stephanie, who had struggled with school and who tended to recede into the walls and become invisible if the teacher wasn't careful. So Judy was always on the hunt for methods that encouraged students to help each other and take on various classroom roles. She wanted to teach for every student's strongest self and to use these strengths to address their own needs and those of other students in the classroom.

Reciprocal reading or teaching encouraged the students to take the responsibility for learning and to help each other. But it also offered Judy the opportunity to intervene and scaffold more expert strategies that might help the students at the point of their need. As in this case, Judy usually started off with students working in assigned pairs (usually a more able and a less able reader, although at this point in the year the assignments were somewhat guesswork). Later in the year, when students were a little more familiar with the technique, she used groups of four and added the roles of learning listener and supportive critic.

The profile about Corbett was a good one, filled with action-packed anecdotes about tiger hunting and cobras in the bathtub, as well as descriptions of Corbett's rather mundane "real" life as a railroad employee in India. On the next day, students were assigned into pairs, and they chose one of several profiles that they would like to read together as they tried the reciprocal reading technique. There were profiles of movie stars, athletes, people representing various cultural groups, singer Natalie Merchant, and other figures Judy thought would be of interest to her students. As they read, she roamed the classroom helping them to use the strategies of helping, questioning, clarifying, summarizing, and predicting.

Students read a wide range of print and nonprint texts to build an understanding of texts, of themselves, and of the cultures of the United States and the world; to acquire new information; to respond to the needs and demands of society and the workplace; and for personal fulfillment. Among these texts are fiction and nonfiction, classic and contemporary works.

A Student-Created Rubric

When they had completed their reading, the pairs used their journals to write their definition of a profile and its purpose, and tell where one might be found and why people might read one. Judy usually asked students to do all of their informal and daily writing in the journal that they kept for class. That way they had a record of their thinking and a reference to use during discussions.

Judy always consciously tried to be very explicit about what the class was doing and why. Here, she wanted students to justify their answers with evidence. After they discussed their written answers, she asked: "How does your definition account for the important things about the profiles you read?" She told the students: "What we are doing here is defining a profile and its uses. What other times in your life might you have to define something and know its uses?"

On Wednesday, Judy handed out three student profiles that had been written in her class over the past few years. She asked the students to read

Students conduct research on issues and interests by generating ideas and questions, and by posing problems. They gather, evaluate, and synthesize data from a variety of sources (e.g., print and nonprint texts, artifacts, people) to communicate their discoveries in ways that suit their purpose and audience.

them, rank them, and identify, in their opinion, what made one better than the others. "We are building our own critical standards here, people. You are going to decide what makes a profile good, and those will become the requirements for *your* profile." When they had completed their individual rankings, she asked them to come to agreement in small groups. These small groups, in turn, reported to the whole class during a large-group discussion.

In the large-group discussion, Judy recorded the student comments about what made a superior profile:

1. It had a snappy and interesting title.
2. The first paragraph was a story or scene that grabbed the reader. (Judy informed the class that this was known as a "hook," a fact that amused some of the students interested in fishing and led to a short discussion about "setting hooks" and metaphoric comparisons.)
3. The reader could see the profiled character. The group elaborated that this included physical features and clothing and seeing the person engage in favorite activities.
4. The person's favorite or typical surroundings were described.
5. There were short stories (which Judy called "anecdotes") about the person sprinkled through the profile.
6. A profile included exact quotations from the person and people who knew the person.
7. Finally, the class agreed that a profile worked to help the reader to really get to know "the innermost" person, as Nicky phrased it.

Judy counted the seven identified items to be included in a good profile. She told the class that they had just constructed a rubric and that, though they might find other items to include in their profile, this served as a great starting point for their writing.

Students conduct research on issues and interests by generating ideas and questions, and by posing problems. They gather, evaluate, and synthesize data from a variety of sources (e.g., print and nonprint texts, artifacts, people) to communicate their discoveries in ways that suit their purpose and audience.

Students participate as knowledgeable, reflective, creative, and critical members of a variety of literacy communities.

Now the class needed to construct benchmarks for each item.

First, they picked a criterion: the reader could see the profiled character. Then they asked: What will the profile include to help us see the character if the writer has done a great job? What will be included if the writer did an OK job? What might the reader observe if the writer really didn't meet this objective? Once the students had provided descriptions of how well each rubric item was addressed and included, then they would have an evaluation tool that could be used to assess their own profiles! Made in the USA by students!

Judy selected the criterion regarding "seeing the character" for modeling because she thought that was the most difficult one to describe. She explained to the class that together they would write benchmarks for this criterion. The benchmarks were to describe how a profile that met the criterion on levels called "Not yet," "OK," and "Expert" would look and would provide an example.

Judy started with three levels of benchmarks because this was the students' first pass at creating them on their own. The students labeled the three levels themselves. Later in the year, some groups used smiley face variations, symbols, or different kinds of terminology to designate the benchmark levels they composed.

As a class, they argued about the definitions of the three levels and the examples. They compared their definitions of each benchmark level to the profiles they had read and ranked. They argued about what differentiated an OK response from an Expert one and so on. When the class was fairly satisfied with the results of these first benchmarks, they counted off by sixes and divided into groups, and each group took one of the remaining six profile criteria.

Group work was used continually throughout the year, and Judy used different techniques for grouping. Sometimes, as in reciprocal reading when it was important to have particular kinds of students working together, she would assign students to groups. For long-term projects, students applied to group themselves. For daily work such as this, she used various ways to group students by numbering off, using birthdays or last names. The object was to group students quickly, but to make sure they worked with a variety of different people during the year.

Using the student profiles they had just read as general guides for their thinking, the groups created their benchmarks. They then passed their benchmarks around the groups for further revision and discussion. For example, the "title" group came up with these benchmarks, and the next two groups added or changed the descriptions included in the brackets:

"Not Yet": The title doesn't really help you get interested in or understand the person in the profile. Examples: "My Paper" or "My Profile" [or "Joe Smith"]. Or maybe it talks about part of the paper but not the whole thing, like "Joe's Surprising Life" or "My Scary Rollercoaster Ride."

"OK": This kind of title helps you get interested in reading the paper and makes you want to get to know the person. [The title gives some clues about the person and what they are like.] Examples: "Being a Rollerblade Champ," "The Boy Who Rides His Bike Everywhere."

"Expert": This really grabs your attention and makes you want to get to know the person. [The title gives some clues about the person and what they are like.] It [might be] funny, snappy and sounds good when you read it. [There's extra energy in it. It gives some specific information.] Examples: "Randi the Rollerblade Queen and Her Royal Crackups," "The Bicycle Boy and His Trip to Illinois."

After writing the benchmarks, Nate told Judy, "That was cool!"

Judy thought that creating rubrics really worked well for the students for several reasons: because it was a new responsibility for them, because they owned the process, and because the rubrics would be used to evaluate their own work. Still, she reserved the right to add, delete, or change information on the rubrics. If she did so, she would explain why and try to get the class to agree.

At the end of the day, Judy would type up and print out the rubrics. She noted to the students that the rubrics could and should be revised as they learned more about profiles. She encouraged the students to use the rubrics and to think about them as they planned and composed their profiles.

Students employ a wide range of strategies as they write and use different writing process elements appropriately to communicate with different audiences for a variety of purposes.

Throughout the year, the students would create rubrics for just about everything they did in class, and they would learn to do so very quickly. For example, before peer revising and editing the profiles later in the unit, students took about five minutes to help Judy create a complete rubric on the board.

Judy asked:

"What's the strategy or technique?" "Peer revision!"

"What will we observe if someone is doing a good job at peer revision?" "We will see people listening to each other, hear them praising each other, questioning each other, giving advice to each other about the profile . . ." Judy scribbled these notes on the board in a column titled "Expert."

"What will we observe if someone is doing an OK job?" "We might hear someone reminding them to praise what's good about the profile . . ."

"What kinds of things do we not want to hear?" "People yelling at each other, putting each other down, making fun of something . . ."

Quick rubric building like this made sure students were on the same page, shared common expectations and goals for the coming activity, helped to review processes like good listening and group work, and provided a visible reference to help guide them through the activity.

Frontloading

Students employ a wide range of strategies as they write and use different writing process elements appropriately to communicate with different audiences for a variety of purposes.

Judy had attended a National Writing Project (NWP) summer workshop twelve years ago, and it really had been the beginning of her professional growth. She made use of the NWP's philosophy of process writing, and she worked hard to do a lot of what she called "frontloading," "prewriting," or "rehearsal": modeling, defining, constructing critical standards, brainstorming, and building strategic knowledge before students actually began to write.

Throughout her career, Judy had increasingly tried, as she put it, "To do less to do more." She wanted to do a few things really well so that she could help her students get after what she believed were the "Big Issues." In comparison with earlier in her career when she might teach fifteen different units during a year, now she taught only six. That bought her classes time to integrate reading, writing, speaking, and listening into each unit, time to infuse reading and writing workshops into the flow of the curriculum, time to build strategies and apply critical standards, to draft and revise productions.

Students apply a wide range of strategies to comprehend, interpret, evaluate, and appreciate texts. They draw on their prior experience, their interactions with other readers and writers, their knowledge of word meaning and other texts, their word identification strategies, and their understanding of textual features (e.g., sound-letter correspondence, sentence structure, context, graphics).

All of the frontloading took time, but she believed it was worth it as students activated background knowledge and connected their prior experience to the project at hand. This not only motivated them, but helped them—such as here—to experience and internalize both general strategies (e.g., questioning, summarizing, predicting) and specific strategies (e.g., inferring character), and they were guided towards a challenging and successful experience as meaning makers.

Judy wanted students to see learning as a recursive process that continually built towards greater understanding, not as something to be done and forgotten. She wanted them to know that they could pursue and complete big learning projects by working both independently and collaboratively.

As a way of connecting their own lives to those profiled in their readings, and as a way of brainstorming personal information that could be used in their own writing, Judy started the second full week of school with a game called Three Stories. In this game, which has many variations, participants told three one-sentence stories about themselves: two were to be completely true, and one completely false. The rest of the class tried to guess which story was the completely false one. If they couldn't, the storyteller won and was rewarded by

Judy with a "fete" from her "fete bag," which included some hard candy, bookmarks, chits for books and all-natural sodas, and other prizes. Judy bought these treats herself, and she felt her expenditure was well rewarded by student motivation and appreciation.

Judy used her "fete bag" throughout the year during games and debates and during what she called "fete/post-mortems," when the class evaluated their performance on a particular assignment or project and "the worthy are rewarded, and the rest resolve to improve and re-do their work." Judy also started class every Monday with a short program she called Happy News! Students would report on their achievements of the past week, and she gave out fetes to recognize those students with birthdays, those who had participated in extracurricular activities, or those who had accomplished something or achieved a milestone in their personal lives.

Judy had fielded questions about external versus internal motivation in regards to her fete bag. But to her, it was just another way of asking students to bring and share themselves in class and to be honored and recognized for what they did and who they were.

Throughout the year, Judy tried to use positive devices that the students sometimes found weird and corny, but generally seemed to enjoy. For example, on Fridays, which were often devoted to free reading workshops, students had to enter the classroom holding their free reading materials and calling out "I am a reader!" The class also engaged in what they called "Appreciation," in which they knocked on their desks whenever someone in the class did something really cool or exemplary. The German teacher had told Judy that this was a tradition in German universities, and Judy readily adopted it. Though she started the technique at the beginning of the school year as a way of recognizing effort and performance—especially for students who did not receive much recognition—the students soon began to use the technique on their own as a way of recognizing each other. Sometimes "Appreciations" were loud and shook the desks, but Judy quickly made her expectations about classroom behavior clear to the students. This was a class where there would be fun, and where students took on responsibility to behave.

Judy started the Three Stories game with her own three tales, which she listed on the chalkboard. She wrote:

1. I was an All-American basketball player during college.

   Some of the students asked what being an All-American meant, and when Judy told them it meant you were chosen as one of the top players in America, several students snorted, and Tim said, "She's too short to play basketball."

2. I went parachuting with my college boyfriend, and he landed on a farmer's roof.

   Here the students broke into laughter and Robby yelled, "No Way!" right out loud.

3. I went to my senior prom in a horse and buggy.

"All right, class," Judy explained, "write down in your journal which story you think is the entirely false one."

A moment later the class took a vote. Most students thought the basketball story was false, and the rest thought the parachuting story was bogus. Only one

Students apply a wide range of strategies to comprehend, interpret, evaluate, and appreciate texts. They draw on their prior experience, their interactions with other readers and writers, their knowledge of word meaning and other texts, their word identification strategies, and their understanding of textual features (e.g., sound-letter correspondence, sentence structure, context, graphics).

student correctly sussed out that the real tall tale was the third story about the horse and buggy. The other two stories were totally true! Judy invited the students to ask her questions. The boys especially were fascinated by the fact she was a successful college hoops star. The whole class insisted on hearing her full parachuting story.

She then asked them to use their journal to record a few character traits that these stories indicated Judy possessed and to tell what in the stories made them think so. During the following discussion, Judy pointed out that the class was making inferences—figuring out what something means, interpreting and extrapolating clues, filling in story gaps. She emphasized that this is something expert readers and writers do all the time, and that it is something they would work on throughout the year.

Now it was time for the students to list their stories, first in their journals, and then at the chalkboard. A lot of students balked: "Nothing interesting ever happened to me." "My life is boring!" Judy wondered whether her examples were too dramatic and set too high an expectation. She walked throughout the class exhorting them. "Come on! Everyone has some interesting tales to tell. What about a dream you've had or a goal you want to achieve? What about a scrape or trouble you've been in? What about a success, a failure, something about your family? You could tell about the cultural group you belong to and customs you have." As she went around the class, she read out a few stories she thought were good examples: "My favorite food is pizza with anchovies. Great idea! You could write about a favorite food!"

Throughout the period, students recorded their story sentences on the board, votes were taken, stories discussed. Most of the students managed to fool their classmates and took a trip to the "fete bag." The kids had a blast; there was lots of laughing and story-swapping and "I remember when you did that!" At the end of the class the students clamored to continue the game tomorrow. "We're going to," Judy agreed. "Tomorrow we're going to take a closer look at some of these stories." In the past, she might have pushed on to another activity. Now, by "doing less to do more," she tried to seize on student enthusiasm as an opportunity to pursue some of the big issues she wanted her course to serve. She didn't mind now playing out something she hadn't planned on over the course of a few days.

The next day the students entered the classroom and found a selected list of yesterday's true stories on the overhead:

1. My relative, George Amos Cook, was a cavalry general and fought in the Civil War.
2. My dad fell from a second-story window and crushed my bike.
3. My uncle is a stock car racer.
4. I met Hulk Hogan.
5. My dog jumped from the road and landed on top of our mailbox.
6. I untied my dad's boat and it floated down the lake and over the dam.
7. I want to be an emergency medical technician up in Alaska.

Judy asked the students to read the list of stories, record which ones revealed the writer's personality, and tell how the rest of the stories could be changed to reveal personality. The class generally agreed that numbers 6 and 7 were best at communicating what the writer was like. They felt that the first five could work to reveal personality by adding the writer's feelings or reactions or possible participation.

Judy reminded the students that they had created a rubric that called for an exciting "hook" for their profile. What kinds of things did they find out that were fun and interesting about other people? What other things would they like to know? How could one of the stories they told be expanded into a hook? The class pursued two models, rewriting the sentence stories into full-blown hooks, then began their homework to write a hook for their own profile. They were also asked to list two or three things they would like to know about other people. These lists would be compiled by Judy into a background information survey to be used during the project if students got stuck about what to include in their profiles.

Into the Computer Lab: The Promise of Hypermedia

Almost two full weeks after the beginning of school, the class finally ventured to the computer lab. A finished "hook" was a student's "ticket" to sit at a computer and begin learning how to use the hypermedia program. The few students who did not have a complete hook had to sit in desks to the side of the lab until their homework was completed and checked by Judy.

Students use a variety of technological and informational resources (e.g., libraries, databases, computer networks, video) to gather and synthesize information and to create and communicate knowledge.

Judy and her social studies teammate, Peter, had devised the hypermedia component of the profile project two years ago as a way of introducing the students to hypermedia, which was a tool they wanted to use (and did use!) during an integrated cultural journalism project they pursued together during the third quarter.

A couple of years ago Judy and Peter had attended a middle school summer institute together. One day they went to a session that reviewed the latest NAEP assessments (National Assessment of Educational Progress). They were surprised to hear that Kirsch and Jungeblut (1986) reported that, though the vast majority of young adults surpassed the literacy standards set three decades ago, at least half of today's students were considered "mid-level" literates who could not find or generate information, add to it, connect it to what they already knew, transform it, or communicate it to others. "In other words," Peter observed, "they can't find information, and even when you give it to them, they can't do anything with it because they can't think!" Their district was spending a lot of money on computers, but the information superhighway with all its attendant technology could only extend students' abilities to find, link, and use information if they could perform these operations in the first place!

This really tied in to one of Judy's pet themes: What is literacy and how can we help develop it? She knew that, according to constructivist learning theory, knowledge is "constructed" in socially relevant and socially supported situations. Judy agreed with proponents of this theory that knowledge the students have actively created, experienced, and organized is the basis of all true learning.

Though literacy was once considered the ability to read and write at the functional level, the demands of the modern world had rendered this definition as obsolete as the horse and buggy she hadn't taken to the prom. Judy liked Rexford Brown's (1992) definition of a new literacy called "a literacy of thoughtfulness." This new definition included the ability to represent information in a variety of ways, to think with this information, to think about thinking,

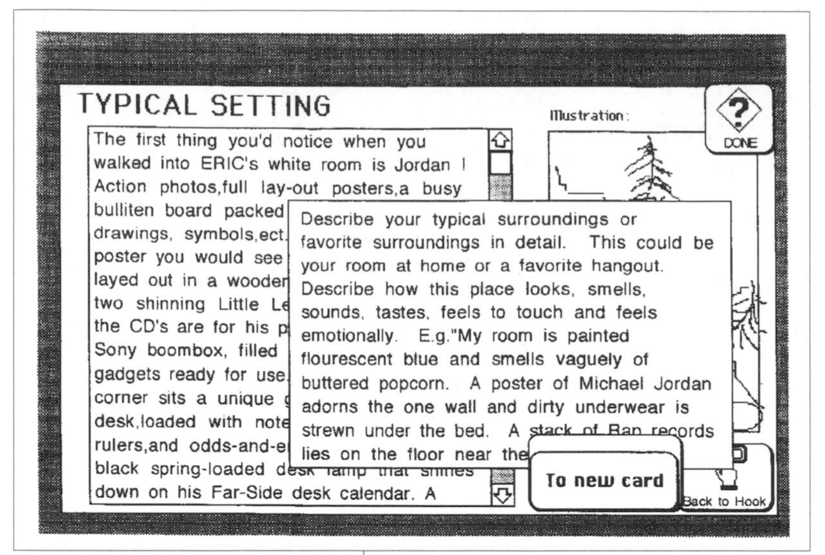

to dialogue with the past and others, to recognize and solve problems, and to use technology to extend these abilities.

The next day Peter and Judy attended a session on hypermedia. Hypermedia consists of computer "cards" that can be filled with information in the form of textual "fields," and a "background" that can be filled with pictures, photos, drawings, graphics, video, music, and voice messages. The cards, which correspond to a page or screen of information, are linked to other cards through the use of "buttons."

Though Judy and Peter didn't much like the presentation, they loved the media and its possibilities. It seemed to them that hypermedia could provide a format that would encourage students to actively engage with various forms of information (text, graphics, pictures, animation, sound), to create, represent, and link that information, and could provide a guide and support as they pursued higher level thinking.

The presentation had demonstrated a hypermedia format that served as an electronic "worksheet." Judy and Peter agreed that this application of hypermedia did not fulfill its promise for helping students to generate and represent information in multimedia form, engage deeply with the information, or reorganize it. They wanted to create a situation where their students could become hypermedia designers, actually using the program to support and extend their abilities as readers, writers, and thinkers. And so it had begun, more than two school years ago. Now, Peter and Judy pursued a curriculum that was largely integrated and driven by a student-design model and that used hypermedia for three projects and some other shorter assignments throughout the year.

That first year, with the help of a former student and true computer aficionado named Jay, Judy created a hypercard template that matched the criteria set by the students. Each criterion became the topic for a card, for example, a title card, a physical description card, one to describe a favorite setting, one to cite what others think of the profiled character. Judy also created a card on which the students reported their literacy and learning autobiography on a scrolling timeline.

On each card there was a space for a visual, aural, or graphic exhibit that could be included to complement the written information about the topic.

Finally, Jay taught Judy how to create a Help button for each card that could provide instructions and examples on what is called a "pop-up field." Judy and Jay decided not to include buttons that linked cards because students could go from card to card with the arrow keys on the keyboard. Then the students could decide for themselves how to link the cards and organize their stack for the reader.

This seemed to be an excellent way to introduce students to the possibilities and tools of hypermedia. The actual cards had been created for them but needed to be filled out. The focus was therefore on helping the students learn how to use all the tools by scanning in photos, creating graphics, recording sound, and eventually creating buttons to link a network of completed cards. Then towards the end of the project, students could actually create new cards and link them to the existing stack.

Students use a variety of technological and informational resources (e.g., libraries, databases, computer networks, video) to gather and synthesize information and to create and communicate knowledge.

But the path of true learning is a scary one filled with pitfalls! Despite all the planning and preparation, Judy found herself constantly asking: Why bother with a computer? There was little institutional support or training available to her, hardware and software came crashing down, and the problems that required immediate solutions took yet more time from Judy's already overscheduled twenty-eight-hour teaching day. Joe took his disk home in his jeans pocket, and it went through the washing machine. Other disks were lost, broke down, or were sabotaged with a pencil. Disk drives went bad, computer programs froze, the fileserver went down. And Judy pulled out her quickly graying hair.

As students were introduced to various hypermedia tools, some were overwhelmed. It seemed like there were thirty hands waving in the air at all times. It was anarchy! Peter and Judy hurriedly put together Help Sheets that they taped next to every computer and to the optical scanner.

Somebody discovered the control panel and fooled with it; there were programming problems Judy had to struggle to understand; the fileserver broke down yet again; and in an unrelated event, Judy's dog got sick. She was ready for some primal scream therapy.

But the problems competed with some obvious pluses. Every day, nearly all of her 130 students had their "entrance ticket," namely, that day's card plan sheet and text, entitling them to work on the computer. And that kind of homework completion ratio was a rarity in Judy's experience.

Students came before school, after school, during lunch and study halls to work on their stacks. They brought in photographs, artwork, video clips, and

HYPERCARD HELP SHEET

STARTING =
1.Turn on computer
2.Insert your disk
3.Double click your disk to open it
4.Double click your stack to open it
5. ⌘ - m to open the message box
6.Type in - set userlevel to 5
7.Press the return key
8. ⌘ - m to close the message box or click on the close box in the upper left corner.

BUTTONS = To make a button:
1.Click on the button tool
2.Pull down Object menu and select New Button
3.A button will appear on screen. To work the button you must double click the button itself.

To delete a button:
1.Click on button tool
2.Press the delete key

To copy a button:
1.Click the button tool
2.Click on button you want to copy
3.Press ⌘ - c to copy button
4.Go to card you want button on with arrow keys
5.Press ⌘ - v to paste the button.

FIELDS = To make a field, delete a field, or copy a field do the same operations described above for buttons except use the field tool.

To type in a field =
1.Click on the browse tool
2.Click in the upper left corner of the field box and type.
3.To change the field operations double click the field (Font, Scrolling, etc.)

TO MAKE A NEW CARD= Go to Edit and highlight new card or press ⌘ -N.

TO SAVE =
1.Pull down the file menu
2.Select save a copy and release
3.Change the name of the stack to what you want
4.Check screen to be sure you save to your disk and to the MacIntosh hard drive by clicking the drive button.
5.Press Save.

TO QUIT =
1.First save.
2.Quit Hypercard in file menu or ⌘ - Q.
3.Close your disk and Hard drive.
4.Drag your disk to the trash can.
5.Go through computer shut down procedure.

KEYBOARD EQUIVALENTS =
⌘ - C = copy ⌘ - V = paste
⌘ - N = new card ⌘ - M = show message box
⌘ - P = print menu ⌘ - Q = quit Hypercard

music to enter into their document. It was so overwhelming that Judy began begging the principal for a computer aide. Hypermedia seemed to be providing a motivation and a context for composing meaning. In her journal, Judy referred to hypermedia as an "empowerment tool" that "is motivating the students and opening up the classroom." Still, she told Peter that before their next project, "We need more support! This was crazy!"

By now, three years later, they had some of that support: a half-time computer aide, faculty members who staffed the lab as an extra assignment, and more inservicing. In the meantime, Judy and Peter had learned something about computers and hypermedia too.

Writing the Profile

Students apply a wide range of strategies to comprehend, interpret, evaluate, and appreciate texts. They draw on their prior experience, their interactions with other readers and writers, their knowledge of word meaning and other texts, their word identification strategies, and their understanding of textual features (e.g., sound-letter correspondence, sentence structure, context, graphics).

This year, for the third through fifth week of school, the class spent about three days a week in the lab and the other two days in the classroom. When in class, Judy taught mini-lessons suggested by the profile criteria. The class went through a short sequence of inference activities to help them build a heuristic—or an outline—of strategies they should use to recognize and interpret clues for making inferences about characters, setting, past and future action, and so forth. First, students worked to understand cartoon characters and their actions, to predict the ends of cartoons, or to fill in missing panels. They completed notes that had been torn in half, inferring from the available evidence who the author was, her purpose, and the note's intended recipient. They told the story of a person's life based on his checkbook stubs. Through each activity they worked on the heuristic, noting the types of clues they should notice and how they could check their inferences.

Students participate as knowledgeable, reflective, creative, and critical members of a variety of literacy communities.

One of the students' favorite inferencing activities during this sequence was called Picture Talk. Judy brought in photographs of people and asked the students to record in their journal who the people were, where they lived, what their job was, what their home looked like, what they did on a typical Saturday night, what they were thinking of as the photograph was taken. After the students discussed their responses and the reasons for them, they began to pair photographs together and imagine a conversation the two might have, paying careful attention to word choice and content. Then a third person would join the conversation. At the end of class, students role played the conversations they had written, much to the amusement of the class, who would critique the language that had been used. For homework, Judy asked them to think about the inferences they had made and whether they were reasonable ones to make.

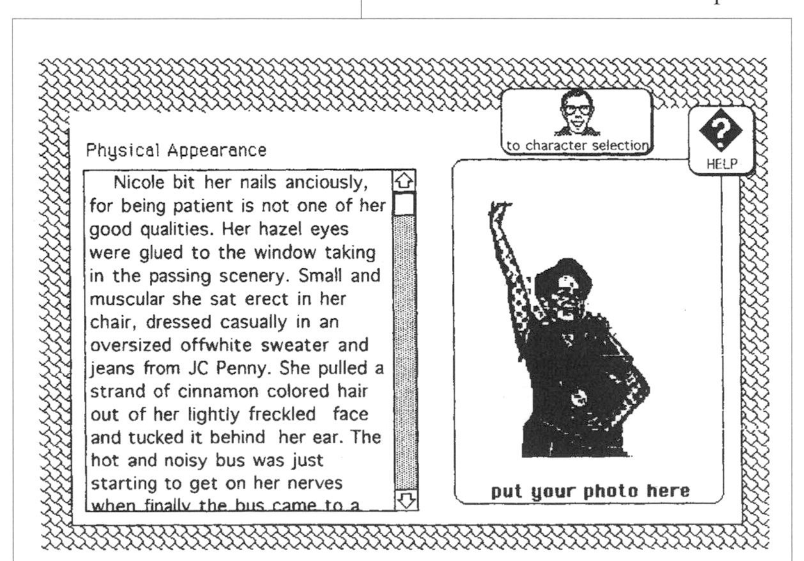

Students discussed the kinds of clues and information they wanted to give their readers through their profiles. What inferences would be made about them?

Besides being highly motivating, the hypermedia program seemed to provide endless new challenges for some students and could scaffold and support other students through various problems. Students like Nicky and Troy quickly completed the required cards and began to create new cards of their own about favorite hobbies, best friends, strong beliefs, and more.

Kae obviously struggled to write her nightly assignment in English. But she was quite an artist, and scanning her artwork onto different cards seemed to help her compose on the attached field. "The picture help me write," she told Judy. "It tell me what to write." Judy changed the hypercard template so that Kae could either scan in one of her artworks or draw a picture with computer tools on each one of her cards. Her peer editors were very impressed with her artwork and printed one of her cards to show their friends. Kae beamed at the attention.

Tim brought in almost telegraphic responses to the card topics. At first, he tried to fill the fields with his nightly writing by making the size of his letters bigger. After deciding that it looked "stupid" that way, he began using the help buttons to generate more material. The layout of the hypercards seemed to help him see that he had not covered his topic sufficiently. The hyperspace seemed to cry out to be filled.

Mike had a different problem. He came in each day with enough text to fill several cards, and much of what he had written was disorganized and off the topic. The nature of the cards, however, seemed to help him see that he had strayed from his central purpose for each card. Because he couldn't fit everything about his appearance onto one card, he divided his information into a physical description card, a clothing card, and a "Mike in action" card that described his "moves" on the basketball court. At other times, while typing onto a field, he deleted material that was off the topic or "less important" as he tried to make sure his information "fit" his current card topic.

Language Workshop for: ______________________________

Noticing!
Study these sentences. What do they have in common? Consider the punctuation and the work it does.

1. Fiona said, "It's not time to go to the lunchroom yet."

2. "I hope that we will do something exciting in reading class today," whispered Jasmine.

3. Tom wondered aloud, "Whoever invented the pizza pocket?"

Coming up with a rule!
What did you notice about the three sentences?

What should you remember about the punctuation?

What is a proofreading key to look for?

Trying it out!
Write out a conversation between Tom, Jasmine and Fiona in which they discuss today's lunch. Be sure to indent each time there is a new speaker, and follow the rules for using punctuation that you just made!

On two separate days, the students peer edited printouts of each other's cards by using their benchmarks, and they devised questions to use as they interviewed their friends and family.

When the cards based on the interviews came due, it was apparent that the students had difficulty using both apostrophes and quotation marks. As a result, a lot of students had trouble reading and understanding who was saying what as they read each other's cards. It was time for a mini-lesson! The students first completed an inductive usage exercise by reading some material that used

Students adjust their use of spoken, written, and visual language (e.g., conventions, style, vocabulary) to communicate effectively with a variety of audiences and for different purposes.

quotation marks to designate dialogue. The students then came up with their own rules for using quotation marks with dialogue. Another inductive exercise examined other uses of quotation marks, for example, to identify titles.

Judy asked the students to read a dialogue-laced short story from which all the quotation marks had been deleted. The class discussed the importance of quotation marks and paragraphing for identifying speakers and understanding what they had said. They reviewed the important rules they had identified about quotations, indenting, and changing speakers, and then they edited the story. Then Judy asked the students to apply what they had learned as they revised their own profiles. She asked each class if the correct use of quotation marks should be added to the criteria, and they all agreed that it should be.

Through the peer editing, students began to keep a running list in the back of their journal of problems they had with usage or spelling particular words. These lists would become personal references that they could use whenever they composed.

Towards the end of the three weeks in the computer lab, Judy taught the students how to create buttons and new cards from scratch. Some students, like Nicky, had already learned how to create new cards, and they served as peer tutors for their classmates still in the neophyte stage. All of the students also created their own links based on how they wanted the audience to be able to proceed through their stack, and individual students created a new card of their own to express another facet of their life or personality not already covered. A couple of students created menu cards at various points in the stack that allowed the reader to choose one of several directions for proceeding.

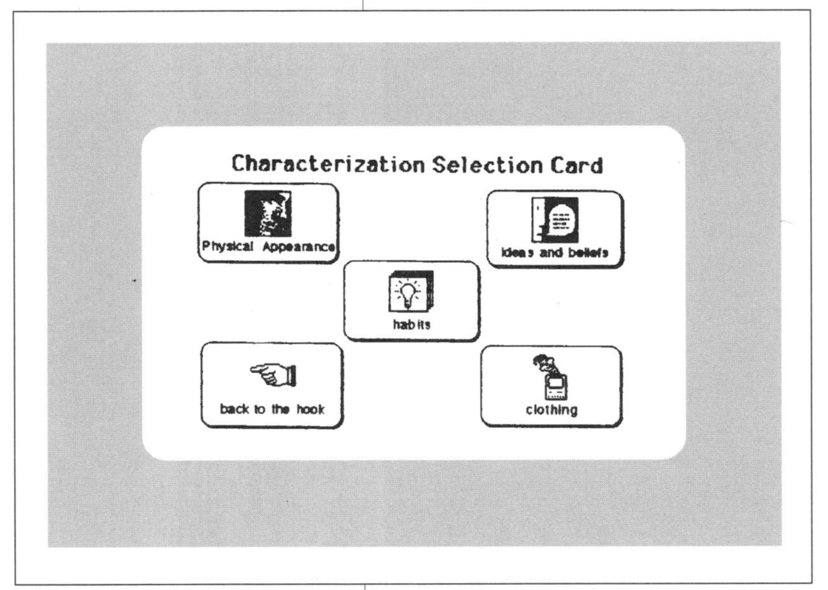

Because things were going well, Judy signed up for another three days in the lab, which—with an additional two days in the classroom—would take the class up to the school's first Open House date. Because she was always looking for ways to infuse poetry into her curriculum, she asked the students to include a card with a poem about themselves. On one day she asked students to write a six-line poem: the first line was their first name, the second line was something they loved, the third line was something they hated or feared, the fourth line was something they wanted to become, the fifth line was a nickname or alias for themselves, and the sixth line was their last name.

Stephanie
lover of horses and riding bareback
she hates taking tests
she wants to be a trainer of horses
(the horses call her) Sugar cube
Sparks

The students then read selections from Whitman's "Song of Myself," and Judy used Kenneth Koch's method of writing poems based on the models of great poetry to help the students write their own "Song." The students started by describing the great things about themselves, the fun and fantastic things they had done—no negatives were allowed! Then they proceeded to tell what they might become and might do, imagining themselves in different places and times, letting their imagination go wild. The students shared their poems and decided together which one should go on their hyperstack and how it could be illustrated. There was a journal writing and ensuing class discussion comparing how the poems worked differently than the prose texts they had been writing. What could the poetry do that the regular writing could not? What aspects of their personality could it capture? When was poetry better than prose? And vice versa?

A few days before the Open House, Judy and Peter put together a letter describing what the students had been doing and inviting the parents to come look through the hypermedia documents. The letter also informed parents about the cultural journalism and video documentary projects that would be pursued next semester, and asked the parents to begin thinking about possible topics and resources with their children. Parents were also invited to come into the school to observe or help out with these and other projects.

The three lab days before Open House were spent peer editing, proofreading, and revising. A problem that continued to recur was telling or listing facts instead of showing a situation or a person in action. Mike wrote: "I love to pig out," but he never described his favorite foods, nor did he show himself eating. Tim avowed: "I am an athletic god," but never showed himself playing any sports. Judy used some of the students' cards to develop a lesson on transforming "telling" into "showing" and making writing a specific experience for the reader.

As peer editors (some of whom were teachers, the principal, or students from other classes) continued to read through the stacks, they evaluated the stacks on the basis of the benchmarks. They also filled out a peer editing sheet

Students read a wide range of literature from many periods in many genres to build an understanding of the many dimensions (e.g., philosophical, ethical, aesthetic) of human experience.

Students apply a wide range of strategies to comprehend, interpret, evaluate, and appreciate texts. They draw on their prior experience, their interactions with other readers and writers, their knowledge of word meaning and other texts, their word identification strategies, and their understanding of textual features (e.g., sound-letter correspondence, sentence structure, context, graphics).

Students employ a wide range of strategies as they write and use different writing process elements appropriately to communicate with different audiences for a variety of purposes.

Hypermedia Presentation
Personality Profile

Answer the following questions. When completed this should serve as an outline for tomorrow's presentation about your hyperstack. You will explain these five answers to the class as you flip through your hyperstack tomorrow.

1. Title Page
Explain how your summary/abstract/call-out sentence is proven in at least two parts of your profile hyperstack:

2. New Card
Explain why you created this card and how it reveals your personality.

Explain the button connection and why this "link" makes sense.

3. Coolest Card (not the New Card)
Explain what you think is your best overall card. Explain why you think this card is particularly interesting and revealing of your personality.

4. What I learned.
Choose three major ideas or processes that you learned from this project. This could be about yourself, about character inferencing or about hypermedia.

5. Improvements.
Explain at least three things you could do to make this profile better and more interesting to read.

Students use a variety of technological and informational resources (e.g., libraries, databases, computer networks, video) to gather and synthesize information and to create and communicate knowledge.

that asked them to come up with a central focus statement identifying the type of personality who had composed the stack. In turn, the authors were asked to add an abstract or summary of the stack to their title card that would "sum up" what the reader would learn about their personality by reading through their stack. In this way, Judy felt that she was continuing to introduce and address important reading skills in the context of what was primarily a writing project.

On the last day of the unit, the students presented their stacks to their third grade reading buddies, with whom they would correspond and share throughout the year. Their part of the schoolwide Open House was a success too, even though some disks were missing and one computer hard drive didn't seem to work. By now Judy felt fairly unflappable and looked on with satisfaction as her students taught moms, dads, and grandparents how to use hypermedia so that they could read through the stacks. The stacks were also printed out and sent to classes at their partner school in the southern part of the state. The partner school students then wrote letters introducing themselves, and commenting on the stacks, to each of Judy's students.

Students adjust their use of spoken, written, and visual language (e.g., conventions, style, vocabulary) to communicate effectively with a variety of audiences and for different purposes.

Looking Ahead

The first unit had been designed to serve several different purposes, one of which was to introduce the students to some ritual structures that would be used throughout the year. For example, the students would help set purposes and would define and construct standards for their projects. They would design and share their own learning projects, using them to teach others. Instruction of specific skills or knowledge–like inferring and reading for central focus, things the class would return to throughout the year–would be embedded in the process of creating the project. And of course the hypermedia design tools they had learned would be used throughout the school year for a variety of learning experiences.

Students read a wide range of print and nonprint texts to build an understanding of texts, of themselves, and of the cultures of the United States and the world; to acquire new information; to respond to the needs and demands of society and the workplace; and for personal fulfillment. Among these texts are fiction and nonfiction, classic and contemporary works.

Students use spoken, written, and visual language to accomplish their own purposes (e.g., for learning, enjoyment, persuasion, and the exchange of information).

As a follow-up to this project, students would be pursuing some free reading during a reading workshop. In fact, on approximately half of the school nights during the year when students did not have an explicit assignment, they were asked to free read at least twenty minutes of any reading material they chose. Judy asked her students, sometime during the next two to three weeks, to revisit the computer room to connect observations and inferences about characters from their free reading to the hypermedia document they had just created about themselves. For example, a description of a character's appearance would be linked to their own appearance card, and a description of Billy's love of his dogs in *Where the Red Fern Grows* might be linked to the student's card about personal interests or hobbies. In this way, Judy hoped, students would be comparing and connecting themselves to characters they met through their reading and would be learning how to create a more extended kind of hypermedia document.

Students apply a wide range of strategies to comprehend, interpret, evaluate, and appreciate texts. They draw on their prior experience, their interactions with other readers and writers, their knowledge of word meaning and other texts, their word identification strategies, and their understanding of textual features (e.g., sound-letter correspondence, sentence structure, context, graphics).

Peter always seemed to get fired up by the success of the profile project and was already busy at work on his lessons for November, when he would ask the students to create a "short stack" on a psychology topic. That assignment would lead into the big integrated cultural journalism project that Judy and Peter planned to do together throughout the third quarter of the school year.

In Judy's mind, the units she taught, both on her own and with others, not only worked toward particular goals, but also intertwined and built on each other, looking ahead to when the skills and knowledge just learned would be applied more independently and in more challenging and sophisticated situations. She tried to help build the students' competence text by text, project by project, experience by experience.

Judy was pretty satisfied with the unit, though she did make some more notes on improvements to be made for the next year. For example, she noted that students should save a copy of their stack to the hard drive each day to protect against lost and damaged disks. And she resolved to lock students out of the control panel.

Still, Judy couldn't help going out with friends to celebrate her temporary departure from the computer room. It sure would be good to get back to paperbacks and pencils for a while! The electronic book had its possibilities, but so did a good old-fashioned book with a direct lineage to Gutenburg!

Some Standards Highlighted

Meaning: Students compose a personality profile representing themselves to their classmates. They use writing, drawing, graphics, and sound through the use of a hypermedia program. Students connect the personalities and experiences of literary characters to their own profiles.

Fluency and control: Students learn strategies for inferring character, setting, time, and missing story details. They learn how to use specific language in concert with pictures, graphs, and other media. They learn how to summarize the meaning of what they have written.

Critical analysis: Students study different profiles and construct their own definition of a profile and critical standards for profiles. They compare and contrast different techniques of presenting a person's character. They review and edit each other's work.

Knowledge acquisition: Students read a variety of profiles to define a profile and understand its uses. They learn how to represent information about themselves in writing and through hypermedia. They learn about their classmates by reading each other's profiles.

Creativity: Students use personal stories, artwork, and hypermedia design features to understand and express their life experiences.

Cultural diversity: Stories from students of different cultural backgrounds are shared through the profiles. Some students read profiles of people from different cultural backgrounds.

Second language: Some students relate personal stories or anecdotes that include terms and phrases from second languages.

Language diversity: Students critique language that people use in different social situations.

Resources

Instructional Scaffolding

Applebee, A., & Langer, J. (1983). Instructional scaffolding: Reading and writing as natural language activities. *Language Arts, 60* (2), 168–175.
Flower, L. (1981). *Problem-solving strategies for writing.* New York: Harcourt, Brace, Jovanovich.
Hillocks, G., Jr. (1995). *Teaching writing as reflective practice.* New York: Teachers College Press.
Johannessen, L., Kahn, E., & Walter, C. (1982). *Designing and sequencing prewriting activities.* Urbana, IL: National Council of Teachers of English.
Lindemann, E. (1982). *A rhetoric for writing teachers.* New York: Oxford University Press.

The Writing Process

Applebee, A. (1986). Problems in process approaches: Toward a reconceptualization of process instruction. In A. R. Petrosky & D. Bartholomae (Eds.), *The teaching of writing: The eighty-fifth yearbook of the National Society for the Study of Education, Part II.* Chicago: The University of Chicago Press and the National Society for the Study of Education.
Berthoff, A. (1978). *Forming, thinking, writing: The composing imagination.* Rochelle Park, NJ: Hayden.
Kirby, D., Liner, T., & Vinz, R. (1988). *Inside out: Developmental strategies for teaching writing* (2nd ed.). Portsmouth, NH: Heinemann, Boynton/Cook.
Macrorie, K. (1970). *Telling writing.* New York: Hayden.
Perl, S., & Wilson, N. (1986). *Through teachers' eyes: Portraits of writing teachers at work.* Portsmouth, NH: Heinemann, Boynton/Cook.
Power, B. M., & Hubbard, R. (Eds.). (1990). *Literacy in process: The Heinemann reader.* Portsmouth, NH: Heinemann, Boynton/Cook.
Rief, L. (1992). *Seeking diversity: Language arts with adolescents.* Portsmouth, NH: Heinemann, Boynton/Cook.

Constructivism and Computers

Brooks, J. G., & Brooks, M. G. (1993). *In search of understanding: The case for constructivist classrooms.* Alexandria, VA: Association for Supervision and Curriculum Development.
Franklin, S. (Ed.). (1992). *Writing and technology: Ideas that work—The best of the writing notebook: Vol. 2.* Eugene, OR: Visions for Learning.
Handler, M., Dana, A., & Moore, J. (1995). *Hypermedia as a student tool: A guide for teachers.* Englewood, CO: Libraries Unlimited/Teachers Idea Press.

Howie, S. H. (1989). *Reading, writing, and computers: Planning for integration.* Boston: Allyn and Bacon.
Male, M. (1994). *Technology for inclusion: Meeting the special needs of all students* (2nd ed.). Boston: Allyn and Bacon.
Means, B. (Ed.). (1994). *Technology and education reform: The reality behind the promise.* San Francisco: Jossey-Bass.
Turner, S., & Land, M. (1993). *HyperCard: A tool for learning.* Belmont, CA: Wadsworth.

Chapter Three

Incredible Journeys: The Drama of Experiencing Story Worlds

Part One: Making Reading Visible

The Challenge to Participate

As Judy considered her second major unit of the year, which would focus on entering into and experiencing story worlds as readers, she knew that she was in for a challenge.

During the first few days of school, as students had completed attitude inventories and reading surveys, Judy noticed that many of her students—and not just those who were labeled—had indicated passive, ambivalent, or downright negative attitudes about reading. For instance, Mike had ranked reading below taking out the trash as a favored leisure time activity! Stephanie had written that "all you do in school is sit and sit and sit and read and get bored." Tim had really cut to the chase as he opined that "reading is stupid!" and elaborated by stating that "anyone who doesn't have anything better to do than read should get a real life!"

While interviewing some of her students, Judy had noticed that most of them regarded reading as something you did to get information—usually information that somebody else wanted. Tim reported that good reading was "answering the questions at the end of the story." When Judy asked if it was still good reading if it were possible to answer the questions without actually reading, Tim gave her a look as if she were impossibly stupid and said, "For sure!" He continued by explaining that you read "to find out stuff for the teacher. If you can find it out without reading . . . that's cool."

Stephanie reported that "I like to read, but it's hard for me and I guess I'm not very good at it because I can't answer the questions and stuff very good."

Trish said that she didn't understand why people "read stories. It's a stupid way to learn things. It's easier to go to an encyclopedia or something."

Even an excellent student such as Troy reported that "reading is a great thing to do when you don't have anything else going on."

Judy was very disturbed by these attitudes. Reading was her passion, and she regarded narrative as a primary mode of mind. Literature, for her, was an invitation and then a dance into her own most secret and innermost heart. Literature was a place to commune with great-hearted and insightful people. A primary reason she had become a teacher of English and the language arts was to share and cultivate her love with a community of readers. So it troubled her that so many of her students regarded reading as something you did to "find out stuff." They seemed to have no inkling that literature could be personally meaningful and held the promise of living through intense, life-opening experiences.

In fact, Judy had begun designing the framework for this particular unit several years ago when she realized that many of her students did not know *how* to live through a story and that she did nothing in class to help them to do so. She realized that most of her teaching had revolved around asking students to reflect on something they had not experienced or understood. In her professional reading, this was a point that several theorists and researchers had made: most teaching and research has focused on the spectator role, in which the reader interprets, evaluates, and reflects upon the evoked world of the text. Little teaching or research has emphasized what readers do to create meaning and elaborate upon it in the role of participant.

For the past three years, Judy had tried to emphasize the participatory dimensions of reading. As part of this project, she had undertaken a teacher research study. In this study she enlisted her readers to identify what stances and moves they used as they engaged with a story. She had incorporated several data-collection techniques into the daily routine of her class. These research tools were designed to provide windows into the mental activity of her readers and to make their reading and thinking visible.

Judy felt that these techniques had been a huge success not only because they aided her in her study, but also because all of her students were able to see what they and other readers were doing, thinking, feeling, and noticing as they read. When her students were able to name what they did as readers, they could celebrate this, manipulate and adapt what they did with awareness, feel more empowered as readers, and set goals to try out new moves they might see their classmates using.

Students apply a wide range of strategies to comprehend, interpret, evaluate, and appreciate texts. They draw on their prior experience, their interactions with other readers and writers, their knowledge of word meaning and other texts, their word identification strategies, and their understanding of textual features (e.g., sound-letter correspondence, sentence structure, context, graphics).

Judy had three rules for her data-gathering techniques: (1) they had to make reading and thinking visible; (2) they had to be pedagogically useful in helping the students to learn about, extend, and share their own reading; and (3) they had to fit naturally into classroom life and be interesting for students to use.

Several techniques were so useful that she continued to use and adapt them after her study and would continue to do so during this current school year. The most successful of these techniques were protocols, literary letters, and symbolic story representations.

It was a powerful move to ask students to research their own reading and learning processes, and Judy tried to layer this element of learning into the portfolios and presentations students used to assess their own growth and learning. She told them right up front that during their semester ending portfolio presentations to a panel of family and friends, they would have to tell what they had learned about how they read and set some goals for improving their reading. Judy told the students that she hoped these research techniques would help them to become more aware of how they read and how to do it better.

Students adjust their use of spoken, written, and visual language (e.g., conventions, style, vocabulary) to communicate effectively with a variety of audiences and for different purposes.

Her colleague Rob had helped Judy get started on portfolios, and he had stressed to her that they should show what students know, how they came to know it, and what significance this knowing has. At first Judy had been disappointed in the portfolios, but Rob had continued to help her, telling her to ask her students, "What makes a difference to your learning, your improvement as a reader and writer? How can you prove this?"

Now, twice a year, Judy scheduled portfolio conferences and had the students invite parents, friends, and classmates. By now her students were aware of portfolio presentations from previous years, and they looked forward to their ten or fifteen minutes of fame out on "the pope's balcony," demonstrating their learning to the adoring masses. Each time they used one of the data-collection techniques, Judy discussed with the students how it could be captioned or explained for use in a portfolio.

Protocols and Journals

Students conduct research on issues and interests by generating ideas and questions, and by posing problems. They gather, evaluate, and synthesize data from a variety of sources (e.g., print and nonprint texts, artifacts, people) to communicate their discoveries in ways that suit their purpose and audience.

Protocols, also known as "think alouds" or "write alongs," were basically a running commentary of mental activity during a composing process, whether that process was reading, writing, or creating an artistic response. Judy used the protocols in various ways throughout the year, including extending them into related techniques such as dialogue journals and dialectical journals.

To introduce protocols, Judy would read aloud to students, stopping at various points to ask them to record in their journal what they were thinking, asking, feeling, noticing, or doing at that point in the story. At other times, students would read a story with carets or stars inserted at a few points, which served as cues to record current thoughts and feelings. She also used a variation of the two-column note-taking technique by copying some stories down the left-hand side of a sheet, leaving the right side blank for students to record or comment on their reading activity.

As students became familiar and comfortable with the protocol technique, many found it easier to respond freely by writing or speaking into a tape recorder as they read, without cues. Judy liked using protocols because they involved all the students and emphasized the reader's activity and experience instead of information to be found. All reading was active, constructive, inferential, and interpretive, and the protocols made this obvious. The protocols themselves were often very rich and offered opportunities to talk about the construction of the text, patterns, themes, the authors of various materials, and much more. Usually, Judy provided class time for students to share and compare their protocols of a particular reading.

Students apply a wide range of strategies to comprehend, interpret, evaluate, and appreciate texts. They draw on their prior experience, their interactions with other readers and writers, their knowledge of word meaning and other texts, their word identification strategies, and their understanding of textual features (e.g., sound-letter correspondence, sentence structure, context, graphics).

It was interesting how the protocols had led to other ways of responding to literature that were variations on a theme. Often Judy would ask students to do a protocol a little differently, and sometimes they would spontaneously adapt the technique. During any particular school year, Judy selected a few rituals, or predictable formats, with which students would become very familiar. They could then innovate, adapt, and extend the possibilities of these structures for their own purposes. With encouragement, Judy found that a few ritual structures provided students with the awareness and means to develop a wide-ranging repertoire of strategies to use in different situations. Creating rubrics for important assignments was a ritual structure. Peer editing and reciprocal reading were rituals. So was her use of protocols, literary letters, and symbolic story representation. After students had been helped to use a structure, they were able to use it naturally and then adapt it for their own purposes.

For example, paired reading and reciprocal reading were two variations on a theme, and these experiences informed students as they assigned roles and worked together for other kinds of group activity. And the protocols were transformed at times throughout the year into dialogue journals, textual glosses, and dialectical journals.

In the *dialogue journal*, a protocol of reading activity and attendant questions was composed down one side of a sheet, and then was shared with another reader. The other reader would then dialogue with the protocol responses by adding observations, answering questions, and commenting on the protocols down the right-hand side of the sheet. Sometimes Judy would dialogue with students in this manner, or she would ask them to take their journal home to dialogue with a parent or sibling. Usually the dialogues were pursued between students, and the class found that interesting dialogues could take place even when the participants hadn't read the same material.

Students apply a wide range of strategies to comprehend, interpret, evaluate, and appreciate texts. They draw on their prior experience, their interactions with other readers and writers, their knowledge of word meaning and other texts, their word identification strategies, and their understanding of textual features (e.g., sound-letter correspondence, sentence structure, context, graphics).

Students adjust their use of spoken, written, and visual language (e.g., conventions, style, vocabulary) to communicate effectively with a variety of audiences and for different purposes.

Protocol and Dialogue Response Example

As Mike read Donald Westlake's "The Winner," about a political dissident who refuses to cooperate with authorities trying to control him, he recorded the following questions and observations, among many others. In the story, the poet Revell repeatedly attempts to escape his prison, though a black box implanted in his body causes him intolerable pain as he distances himself from his jail cell.

Students read a wide range of literature from many periods in many genres to build an understanding of the many dimensions (e.g., philosophical, ethical, aesthetic) of human experience.

"Why is he [the main character Revell] in jail?"

"What does writing poetry have to do with anything?"

"I feel like I'm out there lying in the grass with him, in total pain."

"Now I'm in the hospital bed next to him and I want to spit on the warden."

"These people are animals! They'll do anything to get their way! You can't control what people think!"

"I wonder when and where this story happens."

When Troy read Mike's protocol observations from "The Winner," he dialogued with each of them in order. He first commented that "I think Revell wrote poetry that was against the government. That's why he's in jail."

"I feel the same way, except I feel like I'm leaning over him trying to help him get up and away from the guards."

"I feel like I'm behind the warden and I want to kick him. He's such a jerk! I wonder how the author makes me feel so much anger?"

"It makes me wonder why people try to control each other or make other people do certain things. It makes me think of the lunchroom and people teasing or being mean."

"I think the author wrote this story to warn us about the future and what can happen if we don't respect differences of opinion or if we try to control people too much, like in school sometimes."

Here, Troy dialogued with Mike's original protocol responses, comparing them with his own responses and building upon these, by answering and asking further questions.

Students apply a wide range of strategies to comprehend, interpret, evaluate, and appreciate texts. They draw on their prior experience, their interactions with other readers and writers, their knowledge of word meaning and other texts, their word identification strategies, and their understanding of textual features (e.g., sound-letter correspondence, sentence structure, context, graphics).

At times, the dialogue journal became a *dialectical journal* (Berthoff, 1981), or a way of conversing with one's own responses. On the left side of the sheet was the protocol, which might include favorite quotations, important facts to be remembered, memories that had been stimulated, a scene summary, speculations, inferences, judgments, questions, and other such observations. After reading, the student would revisit the entries by commenting on them with further questions, interpretations, and evaluations.

Sometimes, when reading unfamiliar or difficult material, students would turn the protocol into a kind of textual *gloss* in which they defined terms, created a context for understanding, connected the reading to previous readings and experiences in the class, and predicted how what they were learning might be useful to a project they were working on.

All of these protocol-related techniques were good ways for students to record and share the free reading that was their usual nightly assignment. Judy asked that students keep some sort of record of their free reading, which she reviewed and responded to each week. The protocols and literary letters were favorite ways for students to "keep track."

These techniques were highly efficient and reinforced an attitude and stance towards the reader as an active maker and monitor of personal meanings that could be shared and negotiated with others.

Literary Letters

Literary letters were another ritual Judy found useful. This was an idea she had found in the work of Nancie Atwell (1987) and her work on the reading and writing workshop.

Though students were usually free to write letters about whatever they liked and to whomever they liked, sometimes Judy asked them to consider writing about a particular question or prompt. This was a way that she could get them to consider new issues and to challenge their reading in particular ways. She had come to believe that general skills of reading were certainly used in every situation (comprehending, inferencing, summarizing, monitoring, predicting), but also that special strategies were required with particular genres and situations (e.g., for reading manuals, following directions, understanding irony, judging narrator reliability). For this reason, she knew that reading a lot was the best way to become a better reader, but she regarded reading experience as a necessary though not entirely sufficient condition for improved reading. For Judy, the mantra "reading is reading" did not fit, and so she tried to help students develop the ability to monitor their own reading, to recognize reading situations that called for particular strategies, and to deploy a repertoire of strategies that might be required.

Students apply a wide range of strategies to comprehend, interpret, evaluate, and appreciate texts. They draw on their prior experience, their interactions with other readers and writers, their knowledge of word meaning and other texts, their word identification strategies, and their understanding of textual features (e.g., sound-letter correspondence, sentence structure, context, graphics).

She was always trying to help students challenge and extend their own reading. She wanted them to feel a personal sense of agency and to exercise control over their reading. To do so, students had to develop a strategic repertoire that they used with awareness by asking: What are my purposes here? What kind of text is this? Given that, how should I go about my reading?

Using Questions

Primarily as a prompt to literary letters and classroom discussions, Judy found Aidan Chambers's (1985) *"Tell Me" framework* very useful. She would always start her prompts and class discussion questions with "Tell me . . . " which immediately decentered herself as an authority and foregrounded the students' activity and thought. The questions could still be specific enough to guide and focus the students to consider particular types of moves and issues. For example, to help students consider how an author had made use of narrative time, she might ask, "Tell me how long it took for the story to happen." or "Tell me, did we find out about the story events in the order they happened? Do you always tell a story in the order it happened? For what reasons might you tell a story in a different order?" or "Were there things in the story that took a long time to happen but were described quickly? vice versa? Tell me why the author might have told the story this way."

"Tell Me . . ." questions could be used and adapted to highlight a variety of transactions with texts and a variety of ways to respond as readers. Judy wanted her students to know that there were a variety of ways to read and respond, and she wanted to encourage these various responses through discussion questions and literary letter prompts. For example, in her research with her students, she found that highly engaged readers often responded in all of the following ways:

Students apply knowledge of language structure, language conventions (e.g., spelling and punctuation), media techniques, figurative language, and genre to create, critique, and discuss print and nonprint texts.

Entering the world of reading: Tell me, what did you expect of this book when you picked it up? What were your feelings and how did this affect your reading? What did you notice when you first started reading? How was your attention drawn to these items? How did the book fit your expectations or surprise you? What do you know that is helping you understand the reading? What might you need to know more about to understand more of the story?

Visualizing and experiencing the reading: Tell me, what impressions are you forming in your mind of people and places? What pictures do you have in your mind's eye? What kind of details in the story help you to see the reading most clearly? What feelings do you have about the reading?

Relating to people: Tell me, what clues do you have to a character's personality? What do you think the character will do? What problems will she have? What character interests you most? Has anything like this ever happened to you? How might that experience help you to understand the character? What is your relationship to the character?

Connecting life to reading: Tell me, how does what is happening in the reading remind you of your own life? make you think of other experiences and ideas? make you more aware of your own life? How might the story action apply to you? How might you use the ideas and situations in the story to think about your own life?

Elaborating the reading: Tell me, what episodes or information did the author leave out? How did you fill it in? What if X had happened? if Y had not happened? If you were the author, what might you have omitted, added, or changed? What other adventures might these characters have?

Describing the text: Tell me, what part of the reading excited you the most? confused you? surprised you? Did the author purposefully try to do these things to you? How did the text work? How long did it take for the story to happen? Who was telling the story? How does this make a difference to the story?

Interpreting the reading: Tell me, what patterns were created by you and the author? What idea was the author exploring? Do you agree with the author? What ideas of the author's made you say, "Yeah, that's right!" or "No way, that could never be!" What ideas of your own did the story help you realize?

Evaluating the reading: Tell me, how do you feel about how the story was told? What do you feel is the most significant part of the book? How good was it? If the author asked you for suggestions, what would you say?

Reflecting on one's own reading: Tell me, what kind of reader was the book written for? Were you that reader? Could you become that reader? What did you do, notice, feel as you read? What questions do or did you have? What was your reading rate? Did it vary? when and for what reason?

Judy worked hard to help her students pursue different ways of reading and to ask and pursue the answers to their own questions. These ideas of honest, open-ended questioning and personal meaning making were big issues highlighted by the standards that both she and Peter returned to again and again throughout the school year, so essential did they believe they were to becoming a lifelong learner and critical thinker.

Students apply a wide range of strategies to comprehend, interpret, evaluate, and appreciate texts. They draw on their prior experience, their interactions with other readers and writers, their knowledge of word meaning and other texts, their word identification strategies, and their understanding of textual features (e.g., sound-letter correspondence, sentence structure, context, graphics).

Students conduct research on issues and interests by generating ideas and questions, and by posing problems. They gather, evaluate, and synthesize data from a variety of sources (e.g., print and nonprint texts, artifacts, people) to communicate their discoveries in ways that suit their purpose and audience.

Besides modeling and making use of "Tell Me . . ." questions, throughout the year Judy and Peter used a questioning framework based on Raphael's (1986) work on *Question-Answer Relationships*, or QARs. Students were helped to identify and use the different question types and what work was required to answer them. Raphael had identified two general categories of QARs: *In the Book*, which depended primarily on textual information, and *In My Head*, which depended primarily on what the reader brought to the reading situation.

Judy liked the QARs because they too helped students to see that readers engaged in a variety of activities as they read and interrogated a text and that different questions worked for different purposes and required different kinds of thinking. The QAR framework, even more so than the "Tell Me . . ." frame, helped students to generate their own questions.

The first type of question was called *Right There*, and its answer could be found in one general place in the text.

The second kind of question was called *Think and Search*. Peter and Judy identified two subcategories of this type: *Finding the Puzzle Pieces* and *Filling the Gaps*. For Finding the Puzzle Pieces questions, students had to find information from the text that appeared in different places and add the details together. For Filling the Gaps, students had to recognize places where information was missing, think about what kind of information would fit or was implied by the story in this textual gap, and then create an event or details that would fit coherently with the rest of the story.

A third type of question was designated as *Author and Me*. The answer to this kind of question was not in the story. The reader needed to think about what she knew from the world *and* the story to come to a conclusion. Questions about theme and a story's significance or how the story informed a student's own thinking were of this type.

Students apply a wide range of strategies to comprehend, interpret, evaluate, and appreciate texts. They draw on their prior experience, their interactions with other readers and writers, their knowledge of word meaning and other texts, their word identification strategies, and their understanding of textual features (e.g., sound-letter correspondence, sentence structure, context, graphics).

The fourth kind of question was *On My Own*. Again, the answer was not in the story. The story might have suggested the question, but was not necessary to answering it.

Class discussions of reading almost always centered around the students' questions, and they often talked about the usefulness of different question types during class. Judy encouraged them to ask and answer their own questions in their journals and literary letters.

Her students kept their literary letters in their journals with their other written work so that they would have a running record of their reading and learning. Typically, students exchanged letters at least twice a week and sent a letter to Judy at least once every two weeks. Judy had a mailbox for these letters on her desk, and she had set up a mailbox system in class so that students could write to friends in other classes. Students were expected to write a response to each letter they received and return it to the appropriate class period mailbox.

Students participate as knowledgeable, reflective, creative, and critical members of a variety of literacy communities.

The letters, too, became a classroom ritual and a rich source of data about student reading habits. Judy also liked that the letters and their contents captured yet another slice of what real engaged readers do when they share and discuss their reading.

Symbolic Story Representations

The *symbolic story representation* was a technique that Judy was proud of, because she had pioneered its use in the classroom. The idea came from the work of Pat Enciso (1990), which Judy found highly influential. Enciso had been getting at the same question that Judy found so compelling: What do engaged readers do when they read? Enciso had developed a data-collection method called the "symbolic representation interview," or SRI, during which her three case study students created construction paper cutouts of various story elements and events to dramatize what they had read and how they had read it.

Judy had started to use the same technique with only a few of her most engaged readers as she investigated what made their reading powerful and interesting. She wanted to know what they did in part so that she could ask how to help her more reluctant and resistant readers to start taking on some of the same stances and moves and hopefully begin to engage with text in new and more compelling ways. Somewhere Judy had heard that it was the teacher's job to make public those secret things that good readers and writers do, and she had taken this to heart.

Now this was the fun part! When other students, including some highly resistant readers, watched their classmates creating and presenting their representations (which Judy called SSRs), they clamored to be able to do it too! Judy believed that good teaching is opportunistic, and this was an opportunity that she seized with both hands.

At first, she asked students to create cutouts of characters and other story elements that would work simply to dramatize the story action of a piece they were reading. On the first pass, she asked groups of students to dramatize different scenes of the same story. They then jigsawed the scenes together and produced a complete dramatization of the story. Her students discussed their different cutouts, why they made them the way they did, how and why various dramatizations of the story were different, and much more. There was lots of discussion, laughter, give and take. Judy looked on in awe as the students took over the classroom for themselves.

Needless to say, she soon took another pass at using the technique. This time each student chose a story from a menu of six stories that Judy introduced to them. After reading her story, each student created a symbolic representation of it. Judy also asked students to create a cutout of themselves as a reader (see Enciso, 1990) and to layer in to their performance a presentation of what they were doing as readers as they processed the story. In this way,

Students apply knowledge of language structure, language conventions (e.g., spelling and punctuation), media techniques, figurative language, and genre to create, critique, and discuss print and nonprint texts.

the SSR became a dramatization of the story *and* a dramatization of how the reader had read the story.

For a teacher so used to toiling for and celebrating small victories, the results were electric. After watching small groups present SSRs to each other, Judy's student teacher said, "This is the best thing I have ever seen happen in a classroom!"

Rod, an LD-labeled student who was a resistant reader, referred to his story about a temperamental basketball player several times as he created his SSR and asked the student teacher's opinion on several fine points from the story. He created an elaborate set for his story: a basketball court with stand-up stanchions and bleachers. His character cutouts were like chess pieces that could be moved around on the set. As the reader, he made himself into a referee, because "I felt like I was right there in the action!" When asked why he was taking such care (highly unusual for Rod), he replied that he wanted "to get it right!" When asked why, he gave the student teacher a significant look and said, "Because I'm *making* this, and other people are going to see it."

Students adjust their use of spoken, written, and visual language (e.g., conventions, style, vocabulary) to communicate effectively with a variety of audiences and for different purposes.

Students apply knowledge of language structure, language conventions (e.g., spelling and punctuation), media techniques, figurative language, and genre to create, critique, and discuss print and nonprint texts.

His comment echoed two epiphanies Judy had experienced as a teacher. First, students care about what they make. To learn, they must create and share knowledge, and often stories or pictures or other concrete materials provide objects for them to think and share with. Second, students have an urge to share the knowledge they have created, and an audience always makes the learning and performance of it more urgent and purposeful.

And so it went throughout the year, the SSR becoming another ritual structure of the classroom. Each student performed five of them, and some chose to do more for special projects or portfolio presentations. Judy was afraid that the students would tire of the technique, but they did not. With each successive performance, Judy would raise the ante by asking them to include a motif or main idea expressed by the story, a cutout representing the author and her presence in the story, or a representation of a personal connection (which sometimes became a separate SSR) which students were able to make to the story.

Symbolic Story Representation
Evaluation Sheet

1. I understood the story	1 2 3 4 5
2. The central focus fit the details and conclusion	1 2 3 4 5
3. The cutouts really represented the characters and ideas	1 2 3 4 5
4. The cutouts were moved in such a way that I could understand major events, situations, relationships, emotions, et cetera	1 2 3 4 5
5. The reader cutout was used in such a way that I understood what the reader did, noticed, felt as she read this story.	1 2 3 4 5

Praise:

Question:

Polish:

THOR'S HAMMER IS STOLEN

Symbolic Story Representation
Planning Sheet

1. What are the major characters, objects and other items of importance to the story? THOR, HAMMER, LOKI, THRYM HEIMDALL	How will you represent them? THOR; VIKING HELMET HEIMDALL : EAR HAMMER: HAMMER LOKI; BIRD THRYM; SNOWFLAKE
2. What setting(s) are important to the story? THRYM'S HALL	How will you indicate this? THRONE
3. What are the major events (5) or situations that you need to communicate to your audience? 1. HAMMER STOLEN 4. THOR TAKES HAMMER 2. COUNCIL HELD 5. THOR KILLS GIANTS 3. TO GET HAMMER FREYJA MARRY THRYM	How will you show this by moving or manipulating cutouts? USE SYMBOLS
4. How will you represent yourself as a reader? AN EYE	What things did you notice, do, feel, see, compare to your own life or other stories as you read this? I FEEL AS IF I'M WATCHING A STORY UNFOLD.
5. What cultural values did you notice in the story? 1. GOD'S HUMAN, CAN DIE AND MUST USE KNOWLEDGE 2. GOOD BEATS EVIL	How will you represent these? MAKE SURE TO SAY BOTH OF THEM
6. What is the Central Focus? YOU SHOULDN'T STEAL IN THE FIRST PLACE	How will you represent this? SAY: THRYM WAS KILLED BY WHAT HE STOLE.

Students would also adapt the technique to their own strengths and for their own purposes. Adam, who didn't think of himself as much of an artist, began to use pictures he had cut out from magazines and generated on the computer as he performed his SSRs. Ron used "found objects" to represent characters, character traits, and story ideas. For example, he used an orange (inner strength), tortilla (selfishness–"she was all wrapped up in herself"), playing cards (a king, queen, and jack for a dad, mom, and boy), dice ("this is a risky, exciting part of the story!"), and much more. Catherine used drawings which she pasted onto construction paper and Monopoly game pieces. Colin and Jack, two other LD students, followed Rod's lead and began creating stand-up characters that they moved around like chess pieces on elaborate sets that looked like maps or a stage with stand-up props. Colin, who had proven to be a very reluctant reader, loved creating SSRs and confided to Judy and the resource teacher, Matt, that "I do it better than the rest of these guys." He carefully chose and read stories to be shared using this technique. Judy was delighted with his sense of personal agency and achievement and actively encouraged it: "You keep showing people how they can make theirs better!"

Like most school years, that one had been highly exhilarating and exhausting, full of success and yet not perfectly satisfying. Judy felt that she could do still more to both challenge her best readers and to invite her disenfranchised readers into the classroom community. She did feel that the social component of these techniques, and the agency granted to the students who used them, was helping to break the cycle of resistance and frustration many students felt towards the reading act. The techniques also helped to make reading visible and less mysterious to students, encouraging them to name what they could do and to see what more they could try. Judy wanted to keep working hard to extend all of her readers and to invite those who were reluctant ever more into the reading experience.

That following summer, as Judy reviewed the data she had collected as a teacher-researcher, several different kinds of themes began to emerge. But the two most salient findings seemed to be that the reading experiences of her highly engaged readers were intensely visual and participatory. Her most engaged and satisfied readers continually described how they entered into story worlds, sometimes as themselves or as a character, sometimes, as one girl had expressed it, "as an unmentioned detail of the story." Students had described entering the story as "a ghost who can float inside and above people," as "a cloud that can change the color of the scene," as a "giant eye that can see everything and even inside of people." But mostly, the engaged readers felt as if they were *there*, inside the story, as a presence or character who related to other characters, felt and was affected by story events, and often participated and manipulated these events or worked to change a situation.

Judy was excited by her teacher research study and found that the process of being a teacher-researcher improved her level of awareness during classroom work. She told Peter, "We'll get change when teachers experiment and then tell compelling stories that get other teachers to say, 'I'd like to try that!'"

She also felt that a specific technique like the SSR helped her students to meet several of the standards–like helping students to gain meaning from pictures, monitor comprehension, develop awareness of strategies, and exercise strategic control as they make meaning through reading, writing, speaking, and presenting.

Students apply a wide range of strategies to comprehend, interpret, evaluate, and appreciate texts. They draw on their prior experience, their interactions with other readers and writers, their knowledge of word meaning and other texts, their word identification strategies, and their understanding of textual features (e.g., sound-letter correspondence, sentence structure, context, graphics).

Drama and Reading

Partly as a result of her findings, Judy was ready for some more action research. She was going to try yet another way to make reading and thinking visible: drama. She wanted to see what effect drama would have as an intervention, especially with her more reluctant readers. She hoped to share her findings from this project with the teacher research network to which she belonged.

This is what she proposed: to use story theater and story drama throughout the shared reading of a classroom novel. Her purpose: to enliven and make obvious the experience of reading for her students–and to observe carefully to see what happened as a result. Though Judy had made isolated use of drama throughout her career, this would be her first attempt at using drama as an extended activity, and the first time that she had used it as an intervention to support student reading. Drama, she thought, was definitely a part of her teaching repertoire that was underused–and there seemed so many reasons to use it.

First, as her work with engaged readers suggested, it might be a way to help less engaged readers to enter and participate in story worlds.

Secondly, it would be yet another way of making reading and response processes visible. Perhaps this would be another opportunity to emphasize the exciting participatory nature of reading and to share attitudes and moves for that kind of participant involvement. Each year as Judy read the initial attitude inventories and reading surveys, she felt that she could not do enough to demythologize this notion that reading is finding out information for someone else. She remembered that Plato had described slavery as "doing someone else's work," and it was no wonder that students did not read, or find it empowering, if they conceived of it as a form of bondage.

Particularly powerful to Judy this year had been the testimony of Stephanie and her comment that in school all you did was "sit and sit and read and get bored." Judy believed that learning required students to interact both physically and mentally with ideas and materials. She believed that her students were whole organisms and that you could not teach just part of them. As a teacher, her job was to engage them physically, emotionally, intellectually, and socially. To provide for discovery and surprise. To help them assent to and enter into the challenges of learning with their whole self. To do so, she felt that she had to recognize and account for how the intellectual working of the mind is meshed with the emotional, physical, social, and cultural aspects of a child's being.

Judy also knew that information was not knowledge. Powerful learning required a context and a way to use what was learned. For this, students needed to personally connect what they knew with what they were coming to know. They had to see ways in which what they learned could inform how they lived their lives.

Drama seemed to be a way that might help students integrate information, as an experience, into larger personal and social contexts. Drama, she thought, might offer a compelling invitation to engage with a literary experience, and an opportunity to practice and play out different literacy skills, abilities, and ideas. It was a way to try out different ways of acting and being and to live out their consequences. Judy was coming to believe that curriculum needed to be varied, full of opportunity and choice, continually negotiated. Drama seemed to provide for those kinds of possibilities.

As a final consideration, she thought that using drama might build some interest and expertise that students could use as they pursued videotaped news shows and perhaps even a video documentary project that she and Peter had discussed organizing as part of their planned unit on citizenship and civil rights.

As they had begun to feel more satisfied with their integrated hypermedia units and more excited about the concept of student-driven curriculum and student-designed learning, Peter and Judy had talked about ways to further integrate their curriculum and center it on student questions and interests. This year, their goal was to use the first semester to provide the background and framework for a second semester of completely integrated and thematic project work. So they were trying to cultivate tools and habits of thought early in the year that they would return to and entwine through the projects of the second semester. Drama seemed to be a tool that could be used for confronting and expressing ideas in some of the media they had discussed having students create: museum exhibits, illustrated books, video documentaries, and dramatic performances of important historical situations and events.

In fact, Judy and Peter were continually looking ahead to the second semester and preparing students to think about these projects. Already, letters had gone home to parents about the cultural journalism project using hypermedia and about the project to follow, which students would determine and negotiate with their teachers. For the hypermedia project, Peter had already formed tentative groups of students with common interests, and they were brainstorming for particular cultures they might want to study and questions they might ask about these cultures.

Once that was done, Judy would help the students write letters to possible informants and sources of cultural information. Something they had learned in the past was that students had difficulty locating and using primary and community resources if they waited too long to get started with the "finding information phase" of their project. Judy and Peter had begun to use a master calendar so that they could schedule and coordinate their instruction and make sure they were building towards the big issues they had agreed upon. The calendar was a big help, and it always changed as the needs and interests of their students dictated.

Students conduct research on issues and interests by generating ideas and questions, and by posing problems. They gather, evaluate, and synthesize data from a variety of sources (e.g., print and nonprint texts, artifacts, people) to communicate their discoveries in ways that suit their purpose and audience.

Part Two: Drama in Action

Setting It Up!

All of that aside, Judy's current problem was to consider how to set up her current reading unit and the drama work she wanted to include in it. She chuckled to herself as she remembered how, as a younger teacher, her planning had been so structured and linear. She could tell you, with some accuracy, how the year would proceed and what kind of lessons she would probably be teaching during a particular week of the year. Now, her planning was negotiated with students, some of it begun weeks before projects would begin, continually revisited and rethought, and often created on the spot at the point of a particular need. Judy liked Peter's metaphor for teaching as "surfing on the crest of the future's breaking wave," but it had taken a lot of struggle to find a comfort level with it. Even now, on some days she wanted to retreat to the "well-made lesson plan."

Animals/Nature Opinionnaire

List T or F for each of the following statements. Give an explanation for three of your opinions.

1. Animals have intelligence.
2. Animals possess the capacity to love.
3. Animals deserve equal rights with humans.
4. Animals must be protected from cruel treatment.
5. Animals have a strong sense of loyalty.
6. Man is superior to animals.
7. Cures for life-threatening diseases should be tested on animals before they are tested on humans.
8. Animals were put on earth to be used by man.
9. Apes are superior to other animals.
10. All life is sacred.
11. Plants have feelings.
12. Animals are important to the quality of human life.
13. If too many species of animals die out, man will begin to die out too.
14. Animals have extra-sensory perception.
15. Animals are capable of superhuman feats.

Before her students had shared their hypermedia profiles with their third grade reading buddies and enjoyed their final celebration, Judy had sent out an interest survey for a thematic reading unit. Nearly two-thirds of the students had picked "Animals" as one of their top two choices, so she had set out to design such a unit. "Friends and Family" and "Adventure" also rated high. The pickings were slim in the school book room, and Judy settled on *The Incredible Journey* (Burnsford, 1960), which was an adventure that certainly explored friendship between people and animals, and between animals themselves.

Judy had also solicited the students to bring in any materials or artifacts about animals for their classroom study center. Soon there were copies of magazines ranging from *Field and Stream* to *American Pet,* books like *Strange Animal Coincidences, Big Red, Bristleface,* and more; some videotapes on animal care, newspaper clippings about dairy farming and horse shows, some taxidermy, two veterinary texts, children's books, picture books, reference books, and more. Judy added a file of short stories she had collected, including one of her favorites, Joan Aiken's "Lob's Girl."

Students apply a wide range of strategies to comprehend, interpret, evaluate, and appreciate texts. They draw on their prior experience, their interactions with other readers and writers, their knowledge of word meaning and other texts, their word identification strategies, and their understanding of textual features (e.g., sound-letter correspondence, sentence structure, context, graphics).

Judy started off the unit with a prereading "opinionnaire" about animals. She tried to make sure that she was active as a teacher before students read, during their reading, and after their reading. Before their reading, she wanted to help them identify what they already knew about the topic, develop a context for understanding new ideas, ask questions, and start anticipating a pleasurable reading experience.

After the students had expressed their opinions about animals, the class read three poems related to the topic of animal character: a humorous one supposedly written by some monkeys denying any connection to human beings, and two serious pieces. In small groups, students used the opinionnaire to locate some of the ideas these poets had expressed through their poems. On a couple of points, there was lively debate within and between groups striving to reach a decision. As students argued, some drew on their personal experience or said, "I just know this one's right!" Judy reminded them that they were now discussing the viewpoint of the author, not of themselves, and asked them to go back to the poem and indicate, "What in the poem makes you think the author would agree with that statement?"

This was an interesting issue for Judy and one that she had long wrestled with: If readers must construct their own meaning, is any meaning they construct OK? And what about reluctant readers? Isn't any meaning they construct an improvement to be encouraged?

Judy believed that if students were not taught to value and understand the perspective of others, such as an author, then they would never be able to learn from what they read. Reading would instead be reduced to simply looking in the mirror over and over again. The whole power of reading to inform us, help us to enter into new experiences, and learn from other perspectives would be denied. So she worked hard to both encourage and value student responses and opinions, but also to differentiate these from the ideas and opinions expressed by authors. When we read, just as when we converse, it would be rude, if not unethical, not to make every effort to understand what the speakers have to say before attempting to disagree or use their words to support our own positions. Judy wanted her students to be critical readers and writers and to possess the ability to question and resist what they had read. Still, she felt that interrogating or resisting an author's vision depended first upon understanding that vision in the first place. The development of Judy's current position had been greatly influenced by the reader-response theories of Louise Rosenblatt (1978), Wolfgang Iser (1978), and a book on literary theory that she had particularly enjoyed called *Before Reading* (1987) by Peter Rabinowitz.

So when students expressed responses, they were encouraged to examine them and identify where in the text and in their previous experience these ideas had come from.

That night for homework, Judy asked the students to write a journal entry that would tell the story of a relationship involving an animal. Though she encouraged them to write from personal experience, she also allowed them to change the assignment in any way they pleased: to write about a relationship they knew or had heard about, to make up a story—perhaps about a relationship they might like to have with an animal, to tell a story about a relationship between animals—or anything else they wanted to do as a variation on this theme.

The next day, the students shared their stories in small groups and noted points of comparison. They discussed how the stories indicated their agreement or disagreement with various statements from the opinionnaire.

Next, the students read two companion pieces debating the issue of animal rights. Students recorded protocol responses about the readings, and then engaged in an initial drama activity. In this activity, the students voted with their feet by standing in a line that formed a physical continuum of their opinions. On one end of the continuum were students who completely agreed that animals should be guaranteed the same rights as human beings, and on the other end were students who believed that animals possessed no rights whatsoever. In the middle were students who were unsure or who felt that animals had no intrinsic rights, but that they should be protected and provided for by humans. In order to situate themselves on the continuum, students had to discuss their opinions with each other.

When the continuum was complete, Judy started a brief drama she called "Call-In Radio." She asked students standing next to each other to respond to certain problem statements and questions that she read out and to discuss their opinions "on the air." She then walked down the lineup with a microphone, revisiting some of the questions as she played the part of call-in radio host:

Students read a wide range of print and nonprint texts to build an understanding of texts, of themselves, and of the cultures of the United States and the world; to acquire new information; to respond to the needs and demands of society and the workplace; and for personal fulfillment. Among these texts are fiction and nonfiction, classic and contemporary works.

Students read a wide range of literature from many periods in many genres to build an understanding of the many dimensions (e.g., philosophical, ethical, aesthetic) of human experience.

"You're on the air, caller. Do you think animals should be used in laboratories to test the safety of new drugs and medical treatments?" After several of the students had responded, Judy asked the line to fold up so that students from different sides of the continuum would then be discussing some of these issues together.

Finally, she asked the students to vote once again with their feet. As the radio host, she asked the students who had changed their position to explain why their opinion had changed.

In these ways, Judy tried to set the tone that the reading unit would include their own concerns and opinions, which they would use to converse with each other and various authors. The introductory activities also served the purpose of getting the students to express what they thought about the themes to be explored, to anticipate personal connections, and to build interest and the promise of pleasure for the unit.

Students read a wide range of print and nonprint texts to build an understanding of texts, of themselves, and of the cultures of the United States and the world; to acquire new information; to respond to the needs and demands of society and the workplace; and for personal fulfillment. Among these texts are fiction and nonfiction, classic and contemporary works.

Over the next few days, students pursued some shared and free-choice readings that involved animals and friendship. They completed a protocol with one of their readings, exchanged some literary letters, and engaged in some role playing and a *story theater* presentation. For the story theater, Judy read the story aloud as the students sat in a circle on the floor. When she paused, student volunteers would venture into the circle and role play the scene she had just read, adding their own embellishments and interpretations. At first, she had to ask for volunteers and assign roles, but by the end of the story, the students spontaneously got up and acted out the scenes. Most of the students volunteered at some point–some of them several times–and Judy thought that the day had provided a good introduction to story theater, or the spontaneous acting out of a text.

Infusing the Text with Drama

As Judy introduced her students to *The Incredible Journey,* she told them that they would be producing a classroom role drama that would encourage them to enact and experience many of the situations that the main characters of the book would find themselves in. She also explained that they would try a variety of other dramas, like creating tableaux and exchanging postcards as characters, as a way of getting "inside the story" and participating in the story as characters would.

She said that in her experience good readers often felt as if they were in a drama or "story world" as they read, and she described her own participation in a book she had just read, Thomas Flanagan's *The Year of the French.* She told how she had cried at the end because she truly felt that she had lost her best friend, the poet Owen Ruath MacCarthy, whom she had come to know and love throughout her reading of the book. At Judy's invitation, other students shared experiences when they had fully involved themselves in the world of a story or film.

Judy concluded by saying that she would ask students to participate in the dramas and to share the ways that doing the drama were both similar to and different from their experience as readers. They would also think about ways the drama might inform and make their reading of the book richer. She asked if there were questions, and then asked for the students' assent to begin the drama. Since a few students were a bit reticent about joining in, she told them to sit on the side and watch the dramas unfold until they felt comfortable joining in.

Judy had planned what she called a *carousel drama* or series of revolving role play situations. She had learned this and many other drama techniques in a workshop with drama educator Brian Edmiston, who had since become a fast friend. Students would work primarily in pairs to explore or solve a particular problem, or live through a particular event that paralleled a situation from the book. Judy thought the drama would work well because everyone would be involved all the time. And since students would be playing off each other in pairs, they didn't need to be intimidated about performing in front of a crowd. Students would also have the chance to return to the same role in different situations and to experience the multiple perspectives of different roles. Both during and after each daily set of role plays, the students would step back and "explode the experience" by discussing what they had done, what else they could have done, how they felt, what had worked and not worked and why, and anything else that came to mind.

Another decision Judy had to make was whether to enact the drama situations after having read the text, as was the case with story theater, or before reading the text. She opted for the latter. Why? She wanted the students to experience the drama world before experiencing the story world. In this way, she hoped they would have an experience to compare to the book that might help them to enter into the story, participate, understand, and think about it. She also hoped that the drama might provide them with a repertoire of stances and moves to use while experiencing the story world, especially since she was consciously trying to articulate for the students the similarity of participating in a story as a reader and as an actor.

Students apply a wide range of strategies to comprehend, interpret, evaluate, and appreciate texts. They draw on their prior experience, their interactions with other readers and writers, their knowledge of word meaning and other texts, their word identification strategies, and their understanding of textual features (e.g., sound-letter correspondence, sentence structure, context, graphics).

When Judy was studying the reader-response theory of Louise Rosenblatt, one quotation that had really stood out for her was this: "We accept the fact that the actor infuses his own voice, his own body, his own gestures–in short, his own interpretation–into the words of the text. Is he not simply carrying to its ultimate manifestation what each of us as readers of the text must do?" (1978, 13). This direct comparison of reading and drama had provided Judy with some of the impetus for this current project.

Judy set up the dramatic situation by talking the students into the drama world through *guided imagery*. She asked them to close their eyes and imagine that a fog had entered the classroom, causing them all to fall asleep. When they awoke they were in what appeared to be an old hunting lodge. From the roof of the lodge they could see several large lakes, pine trees, and forest for as far as the eye could see, and no roads of any type. An aquaplane bobbed in the water near a large pier. There were several people around who appeared to be guards and who had prepared breakfast for them. The guards appeared to be kind, but did not seem to speak English, as they failed to respond to any of the group's questions. Judy asked if the students were ready to begin participating in the drama world at this point, and when they agreed, she began the drama.

The students decided that the first thing they needed to do was to have a meeting and to decide where they were, why they might be here, and what they could do about it. Mike reported that he had been up on the roof and that there "was nothing but trees." Tim had been down to the dock and said that there "were no keys in the plane. There's no way out that I can see." Judy worked together with Mike and Tim to invite other students into the drama by demonstrating how to act and by asking other students questions. One girl, Diana, began to sob and say that she "missed her family." Several students went over to comfort her. Joe thought that they must be in Canada. "There's no place else with this many trees and lakes–and how far could they have taken us anyway?

Judy asked the students to write diary entries expressing their feelings and any ideas of what they could do to help themselves.

Several students suggested running away, but there was the matter of the guards and of the immense wilderness around them. The group decided to wait to see what would happen.

Judy informed them that over the course of several weeks they were well cared for and fed, but they never received an explanation for their kidnapping. Winter seemed to be quickly approaching and frost was in the air. Then one day they woke up and found they were alone. The guards had disappeared!

The students reentered the drama world, and a town meeting was called to address the following questions: Why are we here? Should we try to find our way home now that we have the chance? And since each class decided to trek across the wilderness in an attempt to reach civilization, safety, and the chance to communicate with home, the classes also asked: What preparations must we make if we are to journey across the wilderness as winter approaches? As a group, what problems do we foresee and what rules do we wish to make for our group?

Each class recorded its list of supplies and rules and made ready to set off across the wilderness of the drama world.

At this point, Judy began to read Chapter 1 of *The Incredible Journey* to the students as they followed along in their own books. For homework, they wrote a literary letter comparing their experience in the drama with that of the animals in the book.

On day two, the carousel drama began. Each student was designated as a role A or as a B. During each succeeding role play, students found a different partner playing the other role so that they could enact the drama in pairs. After two or three minutes of role playing, the students were asked to switch partners and a new role play was begun. These drama scenarios were designed to parallel events in the reading of Chapter 2 and Chapter 3.

Judy informed the students that they had made their way into the wilderness. They had no idea where they were and had seen no people or traveled paths for at least six days. Already, they had nearly run out of food. Role A, though hungry, had some luck hunting and fishing, and still possessed a small cache of food. The students playing role B, however, were weak and starving, not having eaten since the second day of the journey. Role B was instructed to search out a person in role A and ask for some food. The students then role played the scene.

After a few minutes, role A found a new role B for a partner. Role B2 was a friend of the person who role played B1 and was quite worried about her. B2 believed that her friend would die if some arrangement was not worked out to find and share food. During the role play, the two students attempted to work out such an arrangement.

After a third switch, role B3 had found her friend lying unconscious on the ground, skin gray, cheeks sunken, and lips bleeding. B3 confronted role A about what to do.

Judy walked around her different classes as thirteen or fourteen pairs of students role played the drama. She videotaped some of the scenes, and that seemed to lend a sense of seriousness to their work. In three of her classes not a single role A would share their food with role B, though some made promises to enslave themselves to role A, to carry their pack, to pay them after their return to civilization. Some students exchanged rings and other valuables in the attempt to get food.

The three scenes had taken less than ten minutes of class time. The students then stepped back from the drama to discuss what they had done, why, and how they felt about their experience. "I knew I should share the food," Steven revealed, "but I felt so selfish, and so powerful, and I just couldn't do it."

Tim revealed that "I was worried about myself, man. I wasn't going to share. They should catch their own food!"

Stephanie, who had played role B, said, "I couldn't believe it that I couldn't get any food. I was starving and begging and no one would help me. I'm so mad!"

How had things changed when their classmate was found unconscious? Steven "felt terrible. But it was too late. Like I wanted to go back and do it over." Stephanie emoted that "I just wanted to scream 'I told you so!' to those stupid people!" Several students wondered aloud what they would really do if ever caught in such a situation.

Judy reminded the students that when participating in a story it was excellent to feel what the characters would and to ask oneself just those kinds of questions. Still, a drama world was not the real world, so they could do and say things that they wouldn't do in real life to see what the emotional and social consequences would be. She also reminded the students that reading could be very much like being in a drama, and she encouraged them to visualize themselves in a drama world as they read.

Judy read Chapter 2 aloud to her students, and then asked them to read Chapter 3 in reciprocal reading groups.

Each day, the classes continued to create their carousel drama paralleling the story. Each night they reacted to the drama and their reading through their journal writing.

Before reading Chapter 5, the students continued the carousel drama with a series of situations that paralleled the animals' river crossing. Now ten days out on their dramatic journey, the students could see lights up in the sky ahead as they camped for the night. Judy guessed that they were only two days' walk from some kind of town. Unfortunately, they were camped on the banks of a wide and torrential river filled with rocks and whitewater. No easy place to cross could be seen.

First, students paired up to discuss the pros and cons of crossing the river here and now versus searching for another crossing. Next, after crossing the river, the group realized that one of their members was missing. What should they do? This scene was role played in pairs and then with the larger group. After a third switch, pairs role played their meeting with a forest ranger and the group member who was separated from them. The students brainstormed the immediate needs and concerns of each person and then role played their meeting.

By this time, all of the students were active participants in the dramas. Though this was true to different degrees, the kids seemed to know how to enter into the drama world and interact in it and were generally willing to do so. Judy was relieved that there was less resistance than she had anticipated. In

Students adjust their use of spoken, written, and visual language (e.g., conventions, style, vocabulary) to communicate effectively with a variety of audiences and for different purposes.

Students participate as knowledgeable, reflective, creative, and critical members of a variety of literacy communities.

fact, most students seemed to enjoy the playful, imaginative nature of the drama and took to it naturally. She considered how younger children used drama naturally in their play and thought that perhaps she shouldn't be surprised at how successfully this drama was working.

By now, Judy was paying special attention to Stephanie and Tim, and to a couple of other labeled or reluctant students who seemed to have come alive during the drama work. She observed their work each day and recorded her observations in her journal. She videotaped their drama work as often as possible. She took a close look at their literary letters and at two protocols they completed while reading later chapters of the book to see if there were changes in their reading activity. And she conversed with these students and conducted informal interviews with them to see how they were feeling and thinking about the dramas and their reading.

When students seemed to have trouble getting started with a dramatic situation or left their role, Judy would intervene in role with the pair, often taking a position on the dilemma at hand or playing devil's advocate. When Tim said that the group should just press on with their journey and leave their lost partner behind, Judy—as a group member—asked, "What if it were you who was washed down the river? What would you want the group to do then?" And when Stephanie told the forest ranger, "All I want is food and a place to sleep," Judy, in role as a radio dispatcher, said, "Was there anyone else with you? Can you tell us about them?"

Judy felt that her job as a teacher was to help her students grow, and that often meant challenging their assumptions, upping the ante, pushing them a little further, and demanding a little more. She liked to stir up the mud a little, and she found that this was easy to do from her role in a story drama. Students who did not like to be challenged during a normal class exchange reacted much better to such challenges during a drama. It was as if the drama really were a world where you could try out different roles and decisions with some measure of safety.

As the reading of the novel progressed, the students continued the carousel drama, which took five to ten minutes at the beginning of each class. Other dramatic activities were also layered into class.

Students apply knowledge of language structure, language conventions (e.g., spelling and punctuation), media techniques, figurative language, and genre to create, critique, and discuss print and nonprint texts.

For example, the students read Chapter 5 and Chapter 6 and experienced the adventures of Tao the cat after being swept down the river and separated from the dogs. Judy asked the students to *write a missing scene* about the two dogs during this time. She explained that often an author leaves gaps for readers to fill in with their imagination. In this case, the readers were left with several days of narrative time when they had no information about the dogs and their situation.

Tim and Marty wrote and performed a scene in which the dogs discussed what they should do to help Tao find them. They decided to stay their course and take turns barking. In the scene, Bodger worried about what they would do for food now that their hunter and provider was gone.

Stephanie and Diana wrote and role played a sad scene with the two dogs huddled underneath a pine tree in the rain. They discussed how upset they were and what chances there might be that Tao had survived. Luath, the labrador, expressed regret that he had encouraged the river crossing, and Bodger, old friend of Tao, ended the scene by howling his grief to the moon.

In role, students also created and exchanged postcards that pictured and described their greatest adventures during the story.

Towards the end of the book, Judy asked small groups of three and four students to pick out the four most key episodes from the previous three chapters. When this had been decided and justified, the students were to create tableaux of these scenes. The *tableau dramas* were created as students physically or artistically "froze" the scenes as moments in time. The scenes showed physical and emotional relationships and displayed character gestures, expressions, and activities.

Some students chose to draw or artistically depict "snapshots" of their chosen scenes. These they presented to the class with narration to create a tableau drama. Other students decided to act their scenes out physically, freezing them at the climax. After the presentation of each tableau, Judy asked the students to provide a headline or caption for the pictures they had presented.

A highlight of the drama work came before the students read the final chapter about the reunion of the animals and their beloved owners. In the role of the animals, students wrote letters to Elizabeth, Peter, and Dr. Hunter and placed them in the middle of the classroom.

Tim chose to be Luath and wrote a letter to his owner, Dr. Hunter. In part, he wrote: "I can't wait to go hunting with you. I miss the boom of the shotgun and geese honking. Pleese, I hope let's find each other!" This note, Judy remembered, was written by a boy who had repeatedly expressed that reading was "stupid."

Dear Elizebeth,

I really miss you.
I can't wait to see you again.
We've had a lot of adventures
but my most memorable one was
the time that I almost died. We had
to cross a river and right when I
started to swim (you know how much I hate water)
The dam broke and it carried me down
the river. Luath tried to catch me but
the river was going too fast. I nearly
drowned. I must have fainted because
when I woke up I was inside a house
they fed me and a girl took care of me.
I missed the dogs so I left. I ran into
some trouble on the way but I made it
back to the dogs. I miss you. Hope to see you soon!
Love, Tao

Each student picked up a letter written by someone else in the class and circled a word, sentence, or phrase that seemed especially powerful. The students then lined up and read the words they had chosen to create a *choral montage* or *class poem*. Students then discussed which selection would be the best beginning and the best ending, and they worked out a new order to their group poem, trying to link line to line. After several trials, they performed their choral poem for videotape. And it was magic! Stephanie ended her group's poem with the line: "I only want to be home with you!"

The students were so excited by the technique that they wanted to do it again. So they repeated the process, this time writing letters from the perspective of the worried owners, hoping against hope that their pets would make it through the Strellon Game Reserve, where they had last been seen.

The next day, the students watched the videotape of their choral montages and compared their spontaneous readings with the ones that they had planned out and crafted. They talked about the patterns in the poems and how they were created, and how the animals' poem and the poem from the owners seemed to converse with each other.

After their reading of the book was complete, the students played a version of the *"To Tell the Truth" game*. In this game, three or four students would play the part of the same story character. The class, serving as judges, would ask the characters various questions. At the end of the game, the judges voted for who had most convincingly "become" that character through their responses to the questions. After the decision, the class justified their choices and took a look at the kinds of questions that had helped to reveal who had best "become" the character.

Tim, interestingly, disagreed with the class's choice of a best Bodger. He complained that the winner had said, "'Bodger looked better at the end of the trip than at the beginning'—but he couldn't have! He had scars from the bear and he had the fight with the collie! How could he look better?" Stephanie, in choosing the best Tao, said, "The first two [contestants] said the scariest things were the fight with the other cats and being chased by the leopard [bobcat], but I think contestant 3 was right when she said getting washed down the river [was scariest] because that was the one thing where she couldn't do anything to help herself. That's why I chose her [contestant number 3 as the best Tao]."

Instead of a test, Judy asked the class what kind of project they would like to complete as a final activity. They decided to form groups to videotape *a newscast* about *The Incredible Journey.* The students brainstormed aspects of news: features, interviews, reports, weather, sports, public service announcements, advertisements. They then brainstormed issues they thought such a show could and should address. Criteria were negotiated with Judy. And off they went.

Judy told the students that news teams had to work fast to get the news to the people before it was "old" and not "news" anymore. The groups had the end of one class to plan and submit an outline, the next day to write scripts, one day to rehearse and revise and the last day to film their shows. On the next day, students celebrated the end of the unit by watching each other's videos, evaluating them, and eating fistfuls of popcorn that they popped in a giant

VIDEO NEWSCAST
THE INCREDIBLE JOURNEY
CRITERIA SHEET

IN A GROUP OF 3 TO 5, YOU WILL BE ASKED TO PERFORM A VIDEO SHOW AND TAPE IT FOR OTHER GROUPS TO SEE. THE VIDEO NEWSCAST WILL CONSIST OF THREE PARTS: NEWS, INTERVIEW AND FEATURE (CALL IN SHOW, DISCUSSION, MUSIC VIDEO, ETC.) YOU MAY ADD ANY OTHER FEATURES THAT YOU WANT, E.G. COMMERCIALS, MUSIC COLLAGES, EDITORIAL COMMENTARY.

EACH PERSON MUST WRITE TWO SCRIPTS IN THEIR JOURNAL. EACH GROUP MEMBER MUST PERFORM IN AT LEAST TWO SCRIPTS.

NEWS

Each group member should compose one of the following news stories in her journal, then report on it in newsperson news style. You must provide all important details: Who, What, Why, Where, When, How, Importance and people's Reactions to the event. Scripts must be included in your journals as part of your grade. Props, Maps, Re-enactments or anything else you do to make your part of the news more exciting and interesting will help your grade!

1. MAJOR NEWS STORY - The return of the animals
2. EVENTS FROM THE JOURNEY - Report briefly on 5 events from the journey and how you know about them, e.g. the cat was washed down the river; you know about it because Helvi told you. Bodger had an encounter with a bear; you know about it from the claw marks on his shoulder.
3. SPORTS - Expand some event or events from the story into a sports story, e.g. the dogfight with the collie could be tag team wrestling; the river crossing could be reported on as a swimming competition, etc.
4. WEATHER -Report on the weather throughout the journey and how it affected the journey.

INTERVIEW

All group members should help to write the interview script. One member will be the interviewer and will write the questions and help to write the answers. Others will play the part of one of the three main animal characters and will write out the answers. All questions and answers should be recorded in your journal.

1. The interviewer must ask a minimum of 6 probing questions about the character, his personality, feelings, or the events which occured in the book.
2. Questions must require a detailed answer, not simply a yes or no.
3. The character must respond completely to each question. Answers must reflect the best of what is known from the book. Facts must be correct. Answers that require inferencing and interpretation should be based on what is known about the character and events from the book itself.
4. Complete scripts must be included in your journal as part of your grade.

FEATURE

Each show must have at least one feature!

Group members not involved in the interview must write a feature script. The feature could be a call-in show; an editorial commentary on the book, the book versus the movie, the characters in the book, etc.; a man on the street interview; MTV video about the book; a commercial for the book or a product that might have been useful in the book (porcupine repellent, K-rations). Any idea of your own is welcome!

Extra features mean extra credit!

popper they had borrowed from the Student Council.

As Judy considered the drama project, she was fairly pleased with how it had worked. Though she had noted some changes she would like to make when she next used drama, she felt that these dramas had helped the students to see that reading is something that happens "in the reader" versus their previous attitude that reading was something "in the text" or "out there." Drama made it easy to experience some of the productive activities of reading, and both Tim and Stephanie–among others–had demonstrated for the first time this year that they were entering and seeing story worlds, relating to characters, connecting their own life to what they read. Several times during the unit, Tim had compared story events to his own experiences camping, hiking, hunting, and fishing, and he had brought to his reading his own experiences with pets and farm animals.

The dramatic activities, Judy felt, had helped these students to see that reading was something that needed to be created and enlivened instead of something that was ready-made and able to be passively received. Stephanie told Judy that she now thought that "reading is doing something, just like you do stuff in a drama." Stephanie was also excited because in a drama "you do things with your body, and you feel things." She described drama as "telling a story with your body."

Students apply a wide range of strategies to comprehend, interpret, evaluate, and appreciate texts. They draw on their prior experience, their interactions with other readers and writers, their knowledge of word meaning and other texts, their word identification strategies, and their understanding of textual features (e.g., sound-letter correspondence, sentence structure, context, graphics).

Judy was especially pleased that students like these had been invited into the reading experience and had been helped to rethink reading by some of their classmates. Stephanie, in particular, often paired up with her friend Diana. Diana helped set the scene for Stephanie and asked her questions to invite her response in role. Stephanie said that she liked working with Diana "because she helps me to see my part and what I could do. And I like to try to do the kind of things she does as the characters." Diana had told Stephanie that she often felt like she was participating in a drama when she read, and this had impressed Stephanie. "Now I try to act like I'm in a drama when I'm reading." Students like Nicky and Troy had also done yeoman's work inviting and extending the dramatic participation of other students.

Judy wished that she had collected more data for her teacher research study, but the everyday business of running a classroom, responding to 130 different students' daily needs, preparing and problem solving seemed often to curtail her data-collection activity. Still, she was pleased with the drama unit, and she knew that she had lots of anecdotal evidence that the drama was a useful way to extend the reading and other literacy activities of her students. She resolved to do further study on drama when she had the chance.

Part Three: Tools for Organizing and Reflecting on the Reading Experience

There were about five and a half weeks until Christmas break, and Judy decided to use that chunk of time as a literacy workshop. She and Peter had agreed on some general learning processes and techniques that they wanted students to have in their repertoire before beginning the projects of the second semester. The big issues they wanted to really focus on were questioning, finding and creating information, organizing information, and representing information.

During the workshop time, Judy wanted to do some shared readings with a variety of materials and to model some learning strategies. The workshop time itself also would provide students the opportunity to pursue some of their own reading and to use the strategies to answer some of their own questions in the context of that reading. Basically, all the strategies would be ways of *note making* or representing information they had learned.

It was at about this time that a mini-furor engulfed the school and the language arts department regarding standardized test scores and the curriculum. The district's scores were down from the previous two years, and there was concern about what to do to raise student achievement. Though Judy had argued for years against the use of standardized instruments to measure individual learning ("One student guesses *e* and is right, and another picks *b* and has several reasons for it and is wrong, and we think we learned something from the results of the test?"), she knew that test scores were a political reality. The recurring discussion highlighted a particular tension in Judy's own teaching. Was there content that had to be covered? And how directive should her teaching be?

Over the past several years, after her school had been renamed as a middle school, some teachers like herself and Peter had tried to integrate curriculum and center instruction on student interests and needs. Judy believed that teaching decisions were based on teaching situations. Her teaching depended on what her kids already knew and on their present needs. She was beginning to enjoy the freedom to make her teaching opportunistic–responding to an interest or need and pursuing it. She liked to provide situations where students were challenged to discover and learn for themselves. Still, it seemed that her students needed to know and be able to do certain things that were learned best through direct instruction.

Students apply a wide range of strategies to comprehend, interpret, evaluate, and appreciate texts. They draw on their prior experience, their interactions with other readers and writers, their knowledge of word meaning and other texts, their word identification strategies, and their understanding of textual features (e.g., sound-letter correspondence, sentence structure, context, graphics).

Judy thought this was the case with understanding topics, details, and central focus (or main idea comprehension) and how these elements worked together to help a reader make sense of a text. Since the students were currently working on creating short hypermedia stacks on psychology topics in Peter's class, this seemed an appropriate time to do a sequence of assignments that would help them build understanding of these concepts text by text. For social studies, they needed to choose a topic of interest from their psychology unit (parapsychology, dreams, famous psychologists, etc.) to be explored in their stack. Peter wanted a hypercard that introduced the topic to the audience, four to six cards that explored subtopics and specific details of the topic, and a final card that summarized the main idea and importance of the topic they had represented on their stack.

Judy started the activity sequence by showing students collages of photographs. What was the topic of each collage and how could you tell? What idea or element was common to each photo? She used a game show format to pursue this idea. She introduced lists of items and asked the students to identify the common topic they belonged to. A contestant would then stand to identify the topic, and the other students would call out "yea" or "nay." She then introduced lists with an element that did not fit and asked for both the topic and the misfit. By the end of the day, she had asked the students to identify the topics of cartoons and short newspaper articles (what's it about–in one or two words?). She even asked students to identify inserted cartoon panels or sentences that did not fit the topic.

The next day, they continued to read cartoons and were asked to identify the topic (what's it about?), the details (the important events or facts), and the central focus (what's the point?). Different groups discussed and debated their differences of opinions. Judy emphasized that readers would sometimes disagree about a main idea because texts allowed for a plurality of meanings. Readers with different experiences and purposes would find a different main idea. But she still stressed that the main idea had to fit the text's details, and she continually asked: Where in the text and in your experience did this main idea come from?

Student Designed Learning Guide
Finding A Central Focus

Step One: IDENTIFY THE TOPIC OF THE SELECTION
Clues to Topic
a) the title
b) look at the first and last paragraph - the topic is usally named
c) what is discussed throughout the whole selection?
d) the topic must include all major details and events from the selection
CAUTION: not every mentioned detail has something to do with the topic. The topic is the common element or connection between details
e) What do all major details share in common?

Mistakes people make:
The topic you identify might be
a) too general or too big
b) off the mark, missing the point
c) only one detail
d) only some of the details, e.g. maybe you didn't think about the ending

Checking yourself:
a) does my topic give an accurate picture of what the whole selection is about? Was I as specific as possible? After naming the topic, can I now specifically picture in my mind what happened? or might I picture something different that also fits the topic statement? If so, how can I change my topic name to correct the problem?

2. IDENTIFY ALL THE MAJOR DETAILS/EVENTS
Clues that the author wants you to notice a detail:
a) details at the beginning of the selection
b) details at the end
c) surprises, revelations, whenever your expectations are not met
d) Repetition
e) Changes - in character, tone, mood, setting, plot twists
f) A question near the beginning or the end often points to the central focus.

Mistakes people make:
a) a detail can be interesting, but not be a major detail that develops the topic and central focus.

Checking yourself:
a) are all the details related to the topic? How do the main details relate to each other? What point do they repeat or add up to?

3. IDENTIFY THE CENTRAL FOCUS: the point or main idea made about the topic
a) the statement of central focus must make a point about the topic, and cover the whole selection
b) Is the central focus directly stated?
c) Which details helped me decide on the central focus? Why are these details important?
d) the central focus considers how the details relate to one another or lead to one another (what caused or led to what)
e) the central focus statement considers the ending and the final situation

Mistakes people make:
a) the central focus statement is so literal and specific it doesn't allow the reader to apply the main idea to their own life
b) too general
c) true, but misses the point of the selection
d) misses the point
e) only fits one detail or event
f) does not incorporate all details
g) doesn't fit ending and final situation

Check yourself:
What point do the main details repeat or add up to? Is the central focus a statement about the topic? Do you agree with the statement? Why or why not?

At this point, Judy asked her students to build a model for understanding topics and the mistakes they made identifying topics. As students read short paragraphs and named the topics, they identified the following four categories for a topic idea: Too General (too big and could include lots of things that didn't fit the topic), Only One Detail (much too specific and could not serve as a category that included the other details), Only Some of the Details (e.g., not considering the ending), Totally Off Base ("You missed it, dude!"), or Right On! (Perfecto!). The students then discussed clues to a topic of a selection that they should pay attention to and questions they could ask themselves to monitor whether they had done a good job of identifying a topic.

Judy introduced the students to *Pyramiding* and *Issue Treeing*, very similar visual techniques for showing the relationships of ideas. A topic went at the top of the pyramid or tree, and the branches or blocks immediately below were for subtopics. Each subtopic had to be an idea included by the topic above it. Under each subtopic were details of that subtopic. Again, each detail had to belong to that subtopic. Judy compared these techniques to *Power Outlining*, a technique Peter had used with the students, and showed them how each level of the pyramid or issue tree corresponded to a level of the power outline.

Students conduct research on issues and interests by generating ideas and questions, and by posing problems. They gather, evaluate, and synthesize data from a variety of sources (e.g., print and nonprint texts, artifacts, people) to communicate their discoveries in ways that suit their purpose and audience.

At the bottom of the tree, Judy asked students to make a funnel. Underneath the funnel they were to write a central focus statement that captured the meaning of all the details working together.

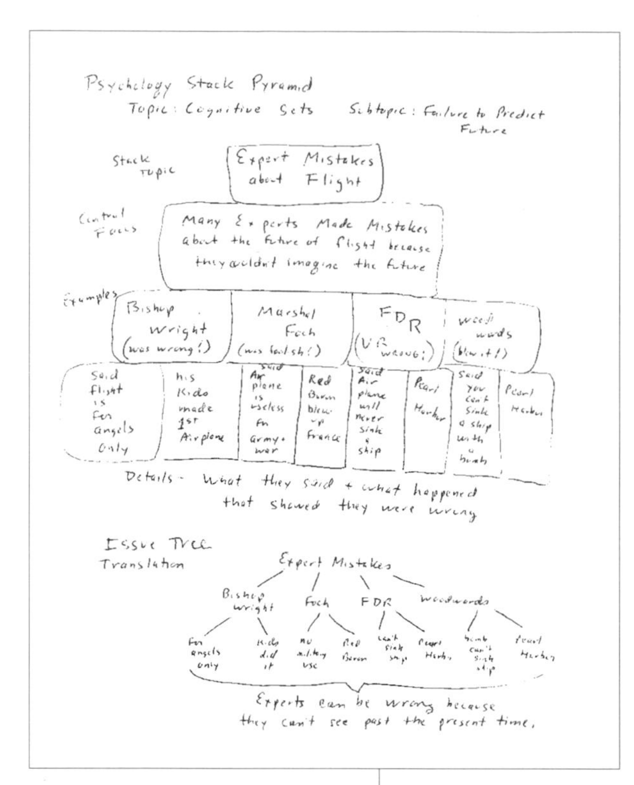

The students then created issue trees for the classes of items found in a grocery store and the library. Once they had understood the technique, Judy asked them to create either a power outline or an issue tree of their planned psychology stack. When they brought it in the next day, they transposed it into the other technique so that they could see the similarities. The similarities and differences, costs and benefits of each technique were discussed.

The students proceeded to read some multicultural short stories and fables chosen by Judy. They identified topics, key details and events, and a central focus or point of each story. In *debates* between small groups, they would argue about what central focus statement was best for each story by relating the statement to the topic and key details.

The kids loved the debates, and Judy had devised a round-robin kind of technique to encourage the students to listen and respond to each other. Each group would decide on a best possible central focus statement for a single story and write it on the board. Everyone in the group had to agree and understand how the central focus addressed the topic of the fable and how the details from the story supported the statement. Proceeding from one group to another, Judy would call on any group member she liked to support the central focus statement they had composed—usually with a detail or inference made from the story. For each detail the group cited in support of their statement, they would receive a point. Other groups could take a point away from the group by showing that the cited detail or inference was in error or did not support the central focus statement. Judy served as the judge, though she discussed and negotiated her thornier decisions with the group so that they could understand her thinking.

Students adjust their use of spoken, written, and visual language (e.g., conventions, style, vocabulary) to communicate effectively with a variety of audiences and for different purposes.

Students participate as knowledgeable, reflective, creative, and critical members of a variety of literacy communities.

The second round of the debate allowed each group to show how their central focus statement, or moral, was better than another group's statement. The group under attack had the chance to defend themselves, and Judy made a decision about whose argument was best. These discussions were very lively, with students often arguing that the other group had made a mistake identifying the real topic or that one particular word in the central focus statement was not the most appropriate one to accurately sum up and interpret the story details.

In another debate, students wrote their own fables and debated the best possible morals in their groups.

Judy hoped that the debates lent a purpose to the study of topics, details, and central focus. She liked that the debates focused the students' attention on word choice and detail. She also liked that the activity highlighted that different meanings could be gleaned from the same text and that there was no one absolute correct meaning. Any central focus statement that accounted for all of the textual features and details was a good interpretation. On the other hand, there *were* interpretations that violated or did not account for all story details, and these had to be found wanting. Judy found that the activity helped her middle level students engage in very sophisticated talk about good reading and valid interpretations.

Judy stressed to the students that reading was both an experience to be lived through and enjoyed and an object to think with and reflect upon. When students identified topics and details and strove to consider significance, they were reflecting upon the experience and construction of the text. The students discussed when a reader might read just for the experience without reflecting on different meanings; times they might read just for information without looking for an enjoyable experience; and times when it would be fun and fruitful to do both.

Students use spoken, written, and visual language to accomplish their own purposes (e.g., for learning, enjoyment, persuasion, and the exchange of information).

By now there were only three and a half weeks to Christmas. Judy was going to have to eliminate some of the note-making techniques for organizing details and getting at central focus that she had wanted to share with her students. Do less to do more! she reminded herself. This was a problem she always seemed to have—trying to do too much.

Judy had been conversing with several of her students who had enjoyed creating the postcards and artistic tableaux during their reading of *The Incredible Journey*. Some of these students were those who had difficulty in school, including Tim and Kae. "We need to affirm these kids and their strengths instead of remediating them," Judy had told Peter. Since these students all liked art, she wanted to introduce some information-organizing techniques that included art.

Judy wanted the techniques to help students generate their own ideas and their own discourse. Since she wanted to use more art, she thought it was time for another pass at the symbolic story representation. The students were asked to dramatize a scene from their free reading or from a set of short stories available on the sharing table. This time, Judy wanted the students to include a cutout of themselves as a reader and to use that cutout to show where they were in the story world and what they did there as a reader. She modeled a scene from her own current reading of Barbara Kingsolver's *Animal Dreams*. She gave the students a brainstorming sheet to fill out and have checked by a partner. They had half of a class period left to prepare, and they devoted their homework time to completing their SSR. The next day, only three students were not ready, and they went into the hallway to finish their SSRs before returning to participate with the groups performing and evaluating each other's work.

Teaching middle schoolers, Judy had a history of students who had trouble getting homework done. Typically she gave students one day to make up missing work before they were "invited" to a homework club during lunch period or after school. If a student skipped that, then a parent was contacted and hopefully some arrangements were made to get the homework done. Judy also used homework as an "entrance ticket" to the class, and students without homework often had to complete it before engaging in the class activity for that hour. This worked particularly well when students were working on the computer, doing a drama or debate, or some other activity that they enjoyed.

Judy asked the students to write about their SSRs and what about them seemed to help them represent and communicate information about their text and their reading. After discussing this issue the next day, she informed the students that they would be learning three more techniques for visually representing information—techniques that would be helpful to them during the projects of the second semester and beyond in the much vaunted Life Outside of School! Whenever she pursued a unit with students, she asked and encour-

Students employ a wide range of strategies as they write and use different writing process elements appropriately to communicate with different audiences for a variety of purposes.

EXPECTATIONS
for
SEMANTIC FEATURE ANALYSIS
RESPONSE ACTIVITY

The purpose of the "semantic feature analysis" response activity is to compare the characteristics of different characters from the same or different books/stories that you have read. You could also use a real person: yourself or someone you know, in the SFA.

The semantic feature analysis could be very similar to the ones we have used in class, but it must include pictorial comparisons of the characters in question. You could also use a different format, such as using columns of pictures to compare characters' qualities, instead of coding devices such as + and -.

STEPS TO TAKE:
1. List the characters you want to compare. Minimum of three.

2. Give a reason why you want to compare them and what you think you will learn from the comparison.

3. List the general characteristics or information that you want to compare. Minimum of seven. Be able to tell why this characteristic will help you to answer the questions you have.

4. Find out whether the characters in question exhibit the cited characteristics or not. Be able to give evidence for each of your answers. In the case that a character changes throughout the book, use the character at the end of the book for your answers.

5. Make your SFA.

6. Add pictures and exciting visual information to make your SFA exciting to look at and easier to understand.

FINALLY:
You will be asked to explain your tree and justify it to your small learning group, and perhaps to the class as a whole.

EXTRA CREDIT:
Add more characters.
Add more characteristics.
Compare to real life characters you know.
Write a prediction of how characters would relate to each other if they met in the future. Write out the scene.
Make it very exciting visually.

Question: Could we have survived the journey described in the book? How do we compare to the animals?

Figure 21
A Blank SFA Grid

Characters / Survival traits	desire to get home	endurance	can catch food	defend self	helps others	can ask for help	sense of direction	can stay warm	brave	can deal w/ problems
Luath	+	+	+	+	+	–	+	+	+	+
Budger	+	–/+	–	+	+	+	+	–/+	+	+
Tao	+	+	+	+	–/+	–	+	+	+	+
Jeremy ✓	+	–	–	–	+	–	–	–	+	+
Susan	–	–	–	–	–	+	–	–	–	–
Tom	–	+	–	+	–	–	–	–	+	+

Answer - Together, the animals had what it took to survive. Together, we probably don't have all the traits it would take to survive

aged them to ask how this kind of work would be important and helpful to them as they pursued their lives.

Judy started by introducing the Semantic Feature Analysis, or SFA. She brought in examples of SFAs from *Consumer Reports, Zillions,* the *REI* outdoor catalogue, and other sources. Students identified some item they wanted to buy and used the SFAs to determine the best buy for their particular purposes. They then created their own SFA for another product they would be interested in purchasing. They listed all of the important qualities to consider across the top and particular models or examples of the product down the side.

Judy then demonstrated how the SFA could be used to answer questions from the students' own lives (Should I go on vacation with my family, stay and act in the summer musical, or accept summer jobs mowing lawns and babysitting?) or questions about literary or informational reading by asking, "Which animal was most important to surviving the journey?" The students were divided between Tao and Luath, with a few votes for Bodger. So Judy asked them to list across the top of the SFA which qualities were important for completing the journey, and the animals' names down the side. They then checked off the qualities that applied. What did they notice? What patterns did they see? Which of the qualities were most important? The students were interested in how similar the animals were in many ways they had not noticed, and though some students still disagreed about the answer to their question, the support for their answers was clearly laid out for them on the SFA.

Judy concluded the lesson by showing some student examples of SFAs in which the students had used artistic icons instead of checks and pluses to indicate the qualities of a character. She then asked the students to create an SFA of their own to answer a question they had about their free reading or about a story from the sharing table.

A couple of days later, after students had had a chance to do some reading, experiment with the SFAs, share them, and conference with her, Judy introduced the students to another technique that she called the *Family Tree*. The family tree was basically a concept map, or web, that showed the multiple relationships of characters to one another.

The family tree could include pictures of the various characters, items associated with them, or their qualities and could use icons and symbols to characterize their relationships or changing relationships with others. Some students even decided to create *Mirror Maps* that would show relationships at the beginning of the story on one side and at the end of the story on the other. This seemed to be a great idea to Judy and she actively encouraged the students to adapt these techniques to their own purposes and questions.

CRITERIA
for creating a
FAMILY TREE

The purpose of the family tree is to show the relationships and connections between the various characters (or forces) in the story or book you have just read.

The family tree could take various forms as an actual family tree, of a semantic map, a power writing scheme, a flow chart, ranking or socio-gram. The one thing to remember is that your family tree should visually show the relationships between characters.

STEPS TO TAKE:

1) List characters
2) Prioritize their importance to the story
3) Identify the puposes each character serves within the story, and for communicating the author's message
4) Identify the relationships between the characters
5) Come up with events or conversations from the text that typify the relationship.
6) Choose how to show the relationships visually.
7) Draw your Family Tree. (You could make notes about why you are depicting the relationships this way in parentheses near the pictures. This could help you when you talk about it to your group.)
8) Add pictures and any other visuals to your tree to make it easier to understand and more exciting to look at.

FINALLY:
You will be asked to explain your tree and justify it to your small learning group, and perhaps to the class as a whole.

EXTRA CREDIT:
Make a mirror map: On the back of your tree, make a family tree of one relationship from your own life that you have experienced yourself or know about that compares in some way with one of the relationships from your family tree about your reading. Be prepared to discuss the similarities and differences and how the book's story of the relationships is similar or comments upon your own real life relationships.

When a group of students asked when they would be reacquainting themselves with their third grade reading buddies, Judy asked them if they would like to extend the tableau drama technique to create picture books for their buddies. The class agreed.

As the students began writing their stories, which would be the final project before the Christmas break, Judy brought in a book cart of picture books from the library. Each day she would read one, and the students would discuss how the pictures contributed to their experience of the story. Judy emphasized that good readers would usually see a story world in their mind. Picture book authors helped the reader by providing some of the pictures. The class then asked these questions: Did the pictures always match how they as readers saw the story? Why or why not? Was this OK? What story details did the artist choose to illustrate and why? What visualizing was left for the students to do even after the pictures were viewed?

The class read *Madeline* and compared the ink drawings with the colorful dioramas. What purposes did the two kinds of pictures serve? They read *Alexander and the Horrible, Terrible, No Good, Very Bad Day* and discussed story structure and repetition as well as how the pictures contributed to the story. After reading *Umbrella,* they discussed *picture mapping,* a note-making technique in which key story details and situations were designated with suggestive icons or symbols. They then created a picture map to summarize the key details of David Quammen's short nature piece, "The Republic of Cockroaches."

After creating their own picture books, they went through a process of peer editing, revising, and polishing. Most of their picture books were Christmas stories like Jack's "Mr. Red and Mr. White Make a Candy Cane." Some were takeoffs on or sequels to books or movies the students had experienced: Tim's "Tintin and the Exploding Christmas Fruitcake," or Troy's baseball adventure

Students read a wide range of print and nonprint texts to build an understanding of texts, of themselves, and of the cultures of the United States and the world; to acquire new information; to respond to the needs and demands of society and the workplace; and for personal fulfillment. Among these texts are fiction and nonfiction, classic and contemporary works.

Students read a wide range of literature from many periods in many genres to build an understanding of the many dimensions (e.g., philosophical, ethical, aesthetic) of human experience.

Students apply knowledge of language structure, language conventions (e.g., spelling and punctuation), media techniques, figurative language, and genre to create, critique, and discuss print and nonprint texts.

"Batman and Batboy." Others were original creations like Nicky's "Invasion of the Chocolate Eaters" or Stephanie's "A Horse for Sugar Cube."

The big issue that came up was one that Judy had not foreseen. What to do with the stories after they had been shared? Some students wanted to give the stories to their reading buddies as presents for Hanukkah, Kwanzaa, or Christmas. Some students wanted to keep their stories for themselves. The group decided that they had to come to an agreement, because it would be unfair for some third graders to get a present while others did not. Eventually, the class decided to leave the stories in the school library to be retrieved sometime in the spring.

On the day before Christmas break was to begin, Judy's students trooped to the elementary school with their stories, which, as Rod said in an indication of his changing attitude toward reading, "is about as good a present you could give somebody."

Judy had to agree, and smiled to herself because some of her students were beginning to realize it.

Some Standards Highlighted

Meaning: Students collaboratively construct and exchange personal responses to literature through postcards, drama, writing, symbolic story representations, and other techniques. Students both evoke and reflect on textual worlds as they read.

Fluency and control: Students actively participate in their reading by using various strategies to experience and then think about their reading. Students use a wide variety of note-making techniques to represent and organize what they experience and learn from their reading.

Critical analysis: Students research their own reading process through protocols, letters, and symbolic story representations to identify and assess their activity as readers. Students represent and organize what they learn from their reading.

Knowledge acquisition: Students learn the moves and strategies other readers use to engage and make meaning with texts. Students learn about animals and their nature and consider the dilemma of animal rights.

Creativity: Students use drama, postcards, and other artistic techniques to enter and manipulate story worlds. They create choral montages and picture books.

Cultural diversity: Students read short stories and fables from various cultures.

Language diversity: Students read some short stories and fables in dialect and discuss how this contributes to the story's meaning.

Resources

Drama in the Classroom

Barnes, D. (1968). *Drama in the English classroom.* Urbana, IL: National Council of Teachers of English.

Bolton, G. (1984). *Drama as education: An argument for placing drama at the center of the curriculum.* Harlow, Essex, England: Longman.

Byron, K. (1986). *Drama in the English classroom.* New York: Methuen.

Johnson, L., & O'Neill, C. (Eds.). (1984). *Dorothy Heathcote: Collected writings on education and drama.* London: Hutchinson.

O'Neill, C., & Lambert, A. (1982). *Drama structures: A handbook for teachers.* London: Hutchinson.

Wagner, B. J. (1988). Research currents: Does classroom drama affect the arts of language? *Language Arts, 65* (1), 46–55.

Wagner, B. J. (Ed.). (In press). *What is learned through classroom drama.* Portsmouth, NH: Heinemann.

Wilkinson, J. (1988). On the integration of drama in language arts. *Youth Theatre Journal, 3* (1), 10–14.

Wilhelm, J. (In press). The drama of engaged reading. *Reading and Writing Quarterly.*

Questioning

Dillon, J. T. (1990). *The practice of questioning.* New York: Routledge.

Raphael, T. (1986). Teaching question-answer relationships, revisited. *The Reading Teacher, 39* (6), 516–522.

Wilen, W. (1987). *Questions, questioning techniques, and effective teaching.* Washington, DC: National Education Association.

Wilen, W. (1987). *Questioning skills, for teachers* (2nd ed.). Washington, DC: National Education Association.

Transactional Theories of Reader Response

Beach, R. (1993). *A teacher's introduction to reader-response theories.* Urbana, IL: National Council of Teachers of English.

Corcoran, B., & Evans, E. (1987). *Readers, texts, teachers.* Upper Montclair, NJ: Heinemann, Boynton/Cook.

Newell, G. E., & Durst, R. K. (Eds.). (1993). *Exploring texts: The role of discussion and writing in the teaching and learning of literature.* Norwood, MA: Christopher-Gordon.

Probst, R. E. (1987). *Response and analysis: Teaching literature in junior and senior high school years.* Portsmouth, NH: Heinemann, Boynton/Cook.

Purves, A., Rogers, T., & Soter, A. (1990). *How porcupines make love II: Teaching a response-centered literature curriculum.* New York: Longman.

Rosenblatt, L. M. (1978). *The reader, the text, the poem: The transactional theory of the literary work.* Carbondale: Southern Illinois University Press.

Sullivan, J., & Hurley, J. (1982). *Teaching literature inductively.* Anaheim, CA: Canterbury.

Classroom Discourse

Cazden, C. B. (1988). *Classroom discourse: The language of teaching and learning.* Portsmouth, NH: Heinemann.

Cazden, C. B. (1992). *Whole language plus: Essays on literacy in the United States and New Zealand.* New York: Teachers College Press.

Hynds, S., & Rubin, D. L. (Eds.). (1990). *Perspectives on talk and learning.* Urbana, IL: National Council of Teachers of English.

Marshall, J. D., Smagorinsky, P., & Smith, M. W. (1995). *The language of interpretation: Patterns of discourse in discussions of literature.* NCTE Research Report No. 27. Urbana, IL: National Council of Teachers of English.

Wells, G. (1985). *The meaning makers: Children learning language and using language to learn.* Upper Montclair, NJ: Heinemann.

The Teacher as Researcher

Branscombe, N. A., Goswami, D., & Schwartz, J. (Eds.). (1992). *Students teaching, teachers learning.* Portsmouth, NH: Heinemann, Boynton/Cook.

Cochran-Smith, M., & Lytle, S. L. (Eds.). (1993). *Inside/outside: Teacher research and knowledge.* New York: Teachers College Press.

Goswami, D., & Stillman, P. (Eds.). (1987). *Reclaiming the classroom: Teacher research as an agency for change.* Upper Montclair, NJ: Heinemann, Boynton/Cook.

Hubbard, R. S., & Power, B. M. (1993). *The art of classroom inquiry: A handbook for teacher-researchers.* Portsmouth, NH: Heinemann.

Schubert, W. H., & Ayers, W. C. (1992). *Teacher lore: Learning from our own experience.* White Plains, NY: Longman.

Shanahan, T. (Ed.). (1994). *Teachers thinking, teachers knowing: Reflections on literacy and language education.* Urbana, IL: National Council of Teachers of English and National Conference on Research in English.

Reading and Writing Workshops

Atwell, N. (1987). *In the middle: Writing, reading, and learning with adolescents.* Upper Montclair, NJ: Heinemann, Boynton/Cook.

Gilles, C., Bixby, M., Crowley, P., Smiley, R. C., Henricks, M., Reynolds, F. E., & Pyle, D. (1988). *Whole language strategies for secondary students.* New York: Richard C. Owen.

Hagerty, P. (1992). *Readers workshop: Real reading.* Richmond Hill, Ontario: Scholastic Canada.

Hobson, E., & Shuman, R. B. (1990). *Reading and writing in high schools: A whole-language approach.* Washington, DC: National Education Association.

McKenzie, J. (Ed.). (1992). *Readers' workshop: Bridging literature and literacy.* Toronto: Irvin.

Meek, M. (1983). *Achieving literacy: Longitudinal studies of adolescents learning to read.* London: Routledge.

Romano, T. (1987). *Clearing the way: Working with teenage writers.* Portsmouth, NH: Heinemann.

Electronic Mail Service

xtar@listserv.appstate.edu

Subscribers to this network include active and aspiring teacher-researchers discussing and planning their work. Hosted by Gordon Wells of the Ontario Institute for Studies in Education.

Teacher Research Journals

King, R. (Ed.). *Teaching and Learning: The Journal of Natural Inquiry*
The Center for Teaching and Learning
Box 8158, University Station
University of North Dakota
Grand Forks, ND 58202

Newkirk, T. (Ed.). *Workshop*
Department of English
Hamilton Smith Hall
University of New Hampshire
Durham, NH 03824

Power, B., & Hubbard, R. (Eds.). *Teacher Research: The Journal of Classroom Inquiry*
College of Education
Shibles Hall
University of Maine
Orono, ME 04469

Chapter Four

Working into the World: Student-Designed Learning on Hypermedia

Building on the Past; Overcoming Obstacles

It was the first school day after winter break, and Peter was pumped up. He gave Judy a high-five as she entered the building.

"This is it, partner!" he exulted. "Hypermedia, hyperactivity, hypertension city! It's all coming down now!"

"Yeah," Judy joked dryly. "And anything with the word 'hyper' in it certainly belongs in middle school."

Through the first semester, Judy and Peter had supported each other's teaching in various ways, but worked primarily in their own classrooms. Throughout the second semester they would be doing more team teaching, often combining classes and working on stations in the library, computer lab, or classroom. Matt, the learning specialist, would also become very involved in their teaming.

This was their third year pursuing a student-designed learning project using hypermedia, and it had become the highlight of the year for Peter. "This is it! This could be the whole curriculum!" he often said to Judy when they were planning, reviewing, or discussing the project. He meant that when students went through the whole process of what they called "student design" they were using all of the cognitive skills that Judy and Peter agreed were important for lifelong learning. And as they did so, they also were gaining content area knowledge on self-selected questions and topics of interest to them. This knowledge was in turn represented in their hypermedia documents and used to teach other groups—both in their own school and in their partner school—about the cultural questions they had asked.

Despite their excitement and belief in the project, they still had a lot of problems to iron out. Peter and Judy agreed that part of the frustration of student-designed projects was that the problems were so visible. When they had pursued more traditional instruction, kids who weren't working or learning kind of blended in, did poorly on the test, and moved on to the next unit. "Anybody not doing their work in this project is kind of totally revealed," Peter had said to her. "They are naked out there in the howling winds for everybody to see." And that was a help as well as a frustration because there was no hiding, for teacher or student. Recognizing the situation, they could then set out to improve it.

Their teaching enthusiasm for the project was interesting in some ways because, as they had prepared this year's version throughout the summer and past semester, they had several times admitted that they had both privately wanted to chuck the whole thing on different occasions. "Sometimes it was so frustrating," Judy admitted. "It was so big and we'd given up a lot of our control."

"Yeah, Jude," Peter agreed, "but *who* do we want to be in control of student learning? This project helps us become facilitators and move away from being dictators. It helps our students take control over their own learning, which is what we want for them anyway. And besides, change is good!" said Peter, mocking a current TV commercial.

Students use spoken, written, and visual language to accomplish their own purposes (e.g., for learning, enjoyment, persuasion, and the exchange of information).

"OK, Peter, but change is also hard."

"Never fear, Jude, because every year we're getting better and better!" Judy laughed at his Norman Vincent Peale imitation.

One thing that was certainly true was that neither would have conceived, pursued, or completed such a big project and big change in their teaching without each other. At a middle school institute they had attended, they had heard that most teaching innovations occurred in pairs of teachers who supported each other and worked together. That had certainly been the case for them. Now they were trying to expand the project to include other teachers. Last year, they had included Matt through the whole process, and this year they would be including the math teacher at a few points where students might want to represent information through various graphs and charts.

Peter liked to say that the process of student design "*is* the process of learning." Already this year, Peter, supported by Judy and Matt, had done a lot of the background work for the project. Students had begun the process by forming groups of two to six students. During the first year, all groups had been made up of four students, but that precluded some students from being in the group they wanted and from changing groups. This year, students had made a topic application to Peter. Kids who really wanted to work together usually requested the same cultural topic, and that was fine.

Peter then formed the groups based on their interests, with an eye to forming good working groups with heterogeneous abilities. He had honored most students' top topic requests, and the second request for all the rest. If a group wasn't working well early on, a conference was held with all group members and solutions sought. Sometimes groups agreed to trade members or form new groups. All in all, the kids seemed pretty happy, and once the project got going the students became excited and started working fairly smoothly together.

The next step was to ask questions about the topic. Rich Lehrer and Julie Erickson from the University of Wisconsin had proven to be invaluable resources to the team as they developed their project. Together they had devised instructional support and student guides for each of the skill areas, like asking questions, that the unit homed in on. The great thing was that the instructional support was embedded in the students' projects, so that it was introduced at the point of their need and supported their current efforts.

Students had brainstormed a variety of questions that reflected their concerns, then evaluated and revised them, and categorized them by using webs or issue trees. An important part of this process was having students present and justify their questions to the class. The class then responded to and critiqued the questions. Something Judy and Peter realized during the first year of the project was that all of the following research, organization, and presentation of

Students conduct research on issues and interests by generating ideas and questions, and by posing problems. They gather, evaluate, and synthesize data from a variety of sources (e.g., print and nonprint texts, artifacts, people) to communicate their discoveries in ways that suit their purpose and audience.

Students participate as knowledgeable, reflective, creative, and critical members of a variety of literacy communities.

Asking Questions: A Guide for Students

Criteria for Asking Questions:

You can ASK if:

- -You begin by asking numerous questions -- brainstorm! [During brainstorming, you don't evaluate your questions--> just generate them].
- -You can use seed questions (who, what, when , where, why, how), especially if you get stuck during brainstorming.
- -After brainstorming, you categorize your questions.
- -Your categorized questions have headings which describe what they have in common.
- -You evaluate your questions to see if they should be refined (like to make the wording more clear, few yes/no answers, combine questions, etc.).
- -Your questions are neither too broad nor too narrow.
- -You evaluate your questions and select a limited number of research questions.

Tips:

1. Pick a topic you are INTERESTED in -- you will be researching it for a long time.
2. Consider the possible answers to your questions --> Are they one word (too narrow)? Can you find information about it (is the question answerable)?
3. When asking questions, keep in mind the task; how are you supposed to present or share the information?
4. After brainstorming, organize your questions and clarify them --> Your questions are the basis of your research.
5. Keep in mind what kind of information you may find.

If Stuck...

- -Use seed questions
- -Change the topic to one you're really interested in
- -Ask a history question (where did something come from, what did it look like when it first started, how has it changed...)

Tips for Categorizing your questions:

- -Think about what is similar about some of the questions.
- -Put the questions that are similar into separate groups.
- -Try to come up with a key word or name that describes each category.
- -Sometimes the categories are subtopics to your topic of interest. If so, this subtopic name could be the name of a category.

information would be question driven. If students did not have good questions that were entirely compelling to themselves and their classmates, then their project would flounder and sink. So the team spent a lot of time in both of their classes on questioning and question critiques. After the *critique sessions,* the groups then further revised and refined their questions. Individual students chose two questions of personal interest to pursue in their research.

"If you think about it," Peter had said to Judy during hall duty one day, "if we just taught them how to ask and critique questions, that would be a heck of an achievement."

In the first year of the project, Judy and Peter had required students to ask questions about one of the cultural institutions–government, education, family, economics, religion–but they had decided that it had very much circumscribed the ideas students could pursue and had limited the possibilities for intense student engagement. It also kept students from studying cultures that were subgroups of a larger culture and that therefore might not have an easily researchable system of economy or government. So the next year and this one, students were allowed to pursue any cultural group and question they liked.

Instead of asking students directly what they wanted to study, they tried to engage the students' personal interests by asking questions like "What things concern you personally? How might that connect to a study of this culture?" "What are your concerns about the world and how it affects you? How might you learn about these concerns by studying culture?"

Going this route meant that sometimes two or three students in the same group might be asking different questions about family life in the culture, or sports and games, or the arts. That had bothered Peter at first because vast elements of the studied culture wouldn't be covered. Now, Peter and Judy knew that there was no way to cover a culture in a hypermedia document anyway. What was important to them was the learning process and for students to engage with an aspect of culture that intrigued them and to understand how the aspect they had chosen expressed culture and was significant to culture. They really wanted students to see that culture was a lens through which people make sense of the world, through which they find, organize, and express meaning. They also wanted their students to develop some appreciation and

Students develop an understanding of and respect for diversity in language use, patterns, and dialects across cultures, ethnic groups, geographic regions, and social roles.

respect for the richness of various cultures and the diversity of cultures that make our world such an intriguing place to live. Besides, since the finished documents were used to teach other students, everyone was provided with a wide variety of information about different cultures and cultural aspects.

Most of all, Judy and Peter wanted the students to feel ownership of the project, and the more choice they could exercise, the more ownership they would feel.

After choosing one or two personally compelling questions, the students had begun the "Finding Information" phase of the project. They had already written letters and made phone calls to solicit information about the culture and to invite cultural informants to school for interviews. A class letter had gone to the editor of the local newspaper, informing the community of their project topics and asking people who could help them to call the school. A survey had gone out to district teachers, asking for reading suggestions regarding the chosen cultures. The students also wrote to the Children's Cooperative Book Center for their suggestions. They conducted electronic information searches and compiled a bibliography of various sources. They had also made any necessary requests for materials through interlibrary loan.

Students adjust their use of spoken, written, and visual language (e.g., conventions, style, vocabulary) to communicate effectively with a variety of audiences and for different purposes.

Students conduct research on issues and interests by generating ideas and questions, and by posing problems. They gather, evaluate, and synthesize data from a variety of sources (e.g., print and nonprint texts, artifacts, people) to communicate their discoveries in ways that suit their purpose and audience.

By now, most groups had one or two interviews scheduled, and most had received information through the mail from an embassy or another organization that represented the culture of interest. As a result of difficulties finding information sources, a couple of groups had changed or revised their topic or their questions. All of the groups had both some primary and secondary sources of information in hand and expected to find more.

A problem the team had experienced the last two years was starting to find information too late. Without a significant amount of information, students could not design their hyperstacks. There had been a lot of frustration and changing of topics when it was really too late to do so. Last year they had started to find information in December, before hitting full throttle and devoting all of their class time to the project when the second semester began. But there were still problems, especially with finding and scheduling informant interviews, so this year they had started the finding information phase in early November.

The informant interviews and presentations were a highlight for all the groups, and a great learning opportunity was lost last year by the three groups who hadn't been able to schedule one. (They conducted phone interviews instead.) By devoting one day a week to the project early on, Peter and Judy hoped that the course of true learning would run smoother through the later phases of the project. And as students gathered information, they were encouraged to make notes using strategies such as two-column note taking, maps, or semantic feature analyses (SFAs).

Though the students would continue to ask questions and to find and develop information throughout the project, they were now ready to pursue the other phases of a student-designed learning process. Beyond *Asking Questions* and *Finding Information,* the design process included the following:

- *Reading and Familiarizing* themselves with the information they had collected
- *Developing* further information through interviews, surveys, and the like
- *Analyzing-Examining* information in detail

- *Organizing* the information pertinent to their question (by using power outlining, issue trees, webbing, or another technique)
- *Designing a Plan* for the stack and for individual cards in the stack
- *Representing* the information to "Show what you know!"
- *Reflecting* seriously on the information and design
- *Presenting* to classmates, teachers, and invited guests, and after these initial presentations and peer editing . . .
- *Refining* the design to make the product more polished, accessible, and interesting to the audience
- *Final Presentations* and making the stacks available to the public–through the elementary and middle school libraries and by sending stack copies to their partner school–concluded the project.

This model of student design, shared with them by Rich and Julie, had been important to Judy and Peter as they thought about a project of this magnitude, which now spanned some four months of the school year from planning to presentation. The model had helped them to conceive of the project, to plan how time and instruction should be spent, and to see where the students were going and how to help them get there.

To help guide the students and to help themselves as teachers to monitor the progress of some 130 easily distracted middle schoolers, Peter and Judy had constructed checksheets for each study phase. So that the students wouldn't be overwhelmed, they worked with one checklist at a time. Each item on the list had to be initialed both by another group member and by Judy, Peter, or Matt. All of the criteria for a study phase had to be checked before students could proceed to the next study phase.

Cultural Journalism Project Checksheet
Asking Questions/Finding Information Phase

All items on this checksheet must be initialed by a teacher before you may proceed to the next phase. Good luck!

_____ 1. Cultural Topic choice = ____________________

_____ 2. List of brainstormed seed questions about topic

_____ 3. List of subtopics of interest to your group

_____ 4. List of brainstormed seed questions about your subtopic choice

_____ 5. Question map of key research questions

_____ 6. Categorize, combine and eliminate subtopic questions to come up with your driving research questions: What do you *really* want to know?

_____ 7. Initial core bibliography of primary and secondary sources.

When all items have been initialed you may proceed to the next study phase!

In this way, students and teachers would know exactly how far along they were and what needed to be done next. This was important because, after the semester break, the language arts and social studies classes combined and students were working with each other and with teachers at stations in different classrooms, the library, or the computer lab. After attendance was taken, students went to the station or area appropriate to their current needs. The checksheets served as a self-monitoring device that helped them know where to go and what to do each day.

Sometimes one of the teachers would take a group on a student-arranged mini field trip. If it was in town, this might be done during school. All three of the teachers also took groups who requested it to the state capital and state university so that they could meet informants, eat an ethnic dinner, and visit a library. These trips were pursued after school time. This was a lot of extra time, energy, and commitment for the three of them, but they agreed that if the students' interest and commitment were there, then they had to match it, step for step.

The checksheets also served as an entrance ticket to the computer lab and provided students with a great motivation to complete the initial phases of the project so that they could start designing on the computer.

This was another problem the team had experienced the past two years: some few students who had little information about their question would be working on the computer. Often, they would design elaborate animations or multimedia displays that expressed little information about their topic, since they didn't know enough about it! Though these students had learned a lot about hypermedia, they had somehow fallen through the cracks as far as content area expertise was concerned. Judy and Peter hoped that the checksheets would help them maintain more rigor regarding the content substance of the project.

Another obstacle in the past was the difficulty of many reading materials that students found as information. Judy had been working fairly hard with Matt on this problem because it particularly affected a lot of the labeled kids. Some of them were reading on a second- or third-grade level, as identified by informal reading inventories. To mainstream them effectively, some adaptations had to be made.

First, the team had begun to collect a library of appropriate reading materials about several cultures, and they then tried to interest certain kids in these cultures. They had also collected some artifacts from these cultures, like magazines, picture books, maps, comic books, recipes, and clothing. They identified videos, art books, and other visual and nontraditional resources. Though they still expected the students with reading difficulties to go through all of the information-finding procedures, it was a help to know that some appropriate materials were on hand.

Because a lot of the kids experienced difficulties at certain points in the project, both with reading and understanding information and with hypermedia design, Judy had been at work developing some other support services. For example, the classes worked on developing *scanning strategies*. She also had enlisted some parents and university contacts as adult tutors to come in on occasion to observe and work with students, sometimes reading aloud with them. For a project such as this, the more people they could use as teachers the better. Peter, in fact, liked to say that the project was working to "deinstitutionalize the school." Judy liked that, and she liked the idea that they were breaking down some of the barriers between school and community.

She believed that a major purpose of school was to open doors to active citizenry. That was easier for students if they could observe and work with citizens who were actively supporting learning. She and Peter had agreed on an open-door policy during the project so that any student, parent, or citizen could come into their classroom or the lab to help support learning. A lot of students from other houses (especially eighth graders who had done the project last year) came in to observe or help out, and though fewer in number, so did some parents and community members. One day, a man from the senior citizen center who had lived in Australia for several years came in, gave an impromptu interview, and then read and critiqued the stacks about Australia. The next day he returned with a jar of vegemite, an Australian cookbook, and menus from several Australian restaurants–all of which proved to be a big help to Joe, who had asked a research question about how the environment of Australia affected eating habits.

Judy had also solicited several eighth grade students who had gone through the project last year to serve as *reading partners* and *peer tutors* during their

Students read a wide range of print and nonprint texts to build an understanding of texts, of themselves, and of the cultures of the United States and the world; to acquire new information; to respond to the needs and demands of society and the workplace; and for personal fulfillment. Among these texts are fiction and nonfiction, classic and contemporary works.

Students develop an understanding of and respect for diversity in language use, patterns, and dialects across cultures, ethnic groups, geographic regions, and social roles.

Students participate as knowledgeable, reflective, creative, and critical members of a variety of literacy communities.

Students apply a wide range of strategies to comprehend, interpret, evaluate, and appreciate texts. They draw on their prior experience, their interactions with other readers and writers, their knowledge of word meaning and other texts, their word identification strategies, and their understanding of textual features (e.g., sound-letter correspondence, sentence structure, context, graphics).

Students adjust their use of spoken, written, and visual language (e.g., conventions, style, vocabulary) to communicate effectively with a variety of audiences and for different purposes.

Students apply knowledge of language structure, language conventions (e.g., spelling and punctuation), media techniques, figurative language, and genre to create, critique, and discuss print and nonprint texts.

study hall times. She had been gratified by the response of many of these students who were eager to share their expertise and help out. Sometimes her readers would pursue reciprocal reading with their group. But because the different group members were usually addressing entirely different questions, students were often reading alone. So Judy asked her students to use a self-monitoring protocol in which they kept a record of questions, difficult sections, or other problems they wanted help with. Then a teacher or tutor would sit down with the student to discuss the selected problems. Because the students had been using protocols throughout the year, they found this technique an easy and friendly one to use.

The tutors and tutees would also often pursue a version of *shared reading* (Copperman, 1986), which was a slight variation on the paired and reciprocal reading techniques. The reader wanting help identified the parts of the selection she wanted to read on her own, and the parts with which she wanted help and support. The pair would then read the selection aloud together, discuss it, and support each other in the requested ways.

Though the questioning and researching had gone well this past year, Judy and Peter agreed that the texts students had composed on their hypercard fields sometimes read too much like reports. In order to encourage the aesthetic crafting of the information to be presented, this year Judy was going to share with the kids a variety of information books that used creative formats and poetic language. These books aesthetically presented information through pictures, overlays, page-activated sound devices, stories, stories told from different perspectives, simple question-and-answer exchange, tours and trips, interviews, alphabet structures, poems, and diaries, all of which were easily adapted to hypermedia. The students also brainstormed other ways to present their information creatively, such as through newspaper or TV news formats, game shows, diaries from people both inside the culture and visiting it, and much more. Rather than viewing informational and literary texts as separate, Judy worked with the students to transform information into creative compositions.

Another concern Peter and Judy wanted to address was the final presentations. In the past, when the groups had finished and combined their stacks, they had made a class presentation and then an Open-House presentation for parents. But the presentations had taken a long time and not everyone in the audience could participate on the computer. This year, they wanted the groups not only to show their hypermedia document, but to have a small learning exhibit featured as well. The exhibit might include a small display of artifacts, some food from the culture, a cultural game to play, a dramatic scene from family life, or something else. Maybe one group member could be helping visitors to tour the stack while other group members engaged other visitors in activities of some sort. They hadn't really figured this out yet, and they had asked their students to think about it too. In some ways, the finished document itself was enough to present, but they wanted another way to represent culture and to engage the younger siblings and others who attended the Open House. It would also provide another way to stress the importance of using primary materials and hands-on engagement–both to the students and to their audience.

Assessing Where We've Come from and Where We're Going

Both Peter and Judy had a few things to tie up before the semester ended. Judy's students, for example, were performing dress-up book reports and making a portfolio presentation about their semester's work. After the semester break, however, Peter's and Judy's classes would be combined, and nearly all of class time would be devoted to supporting the cultural journalism project for about six to eight weeks.

Judy was pleased with the dress-up book reports. She suggested to the students that they might use some variation of these reports during their final presentations of the hypermedia-cultural journalism learning project by playing the part of a cultural informant.

In the dress-up book reports, students reported and acted out a part of a book or story they had been reading on their own. As always seemed to be the case, students transformed the project to their own ends. This was something that Judy actively encouraged throughout the year. Some students performed a monologue or acted out part of their book as a main character, sometimes enlisting a classmate to help them. Some students, like Diana and Stephanie, who had read the same book acted out scenes in groups. A few students performed the book report as the author trying to sell the book, and Tim acted his out as an illustrator who had been asked to provide pictures for the next edition.

Students apply a wide range of strategies to comprehend, interpret, evaluate, and appreciate texts. They draw on their prior experience, their interactions with other readers and writers, their knowledge of word meaning and other texts, their word identification strategies, and their understanding of textual features (e.g., sound-letter correspondence, sentence structure, context, graphics).

Students adjust their use of spoken, written, and visual language (e.g., conventions, style, vocabulary) to communicate effectively with a variety of audiences and for different purposes.

The Family and Friends Portfolio Presentations also went fairly well. Judy liked the fact that they were both ending one semester and beginning the next with assessment. The students and teachers were all asking: "Where have we traveled? And where do we want to go next?"

Judy had tried to make assessment an ongoing practice that was part of every school day. This was one reason for using protocols, symbolic story representations (SSRs), peer editing, presentations, and literary letters: to make visible and assess with students what we're doing, what we're learning, what questions and obstacles we are confronting, and to set goals about where to go next. These were continual opportunities to reflect on learning and set out anew. Judy believed that teaching, learning, and assessment should be so intertwined as to make a single cord of rope.

Judy and Peter also agreed that the purpose of assessment was not to point out student weaknesses, but to provide an opportunity to discover, celebrate, and reflect on strengths and to set personally relevant goals for the future. They both rejected the deficit view of learning that led to the labeling of so many of their students, and they wanted to replace it with something more positive.

They also believed that the purpose of assessment should be to help students build their own critical standards about their work, their learning, and the world. This could not be achieved and students could not become responsible for their own learning unless they became responsible for monitoring and assessing their own processes and performances.

Students participate as knowledgeable, reflective, creative, and critical members of a variety of literacy communities.

Students use spoken, written, and visual language to accomplish their own purposes (e.g., for learning, enjoyment, persuasion, and the exchange of information).

The hard part was that a letter grade still had to be awarded on the quarterly report card, and this was something Peter and Judy negotiated with students.

Some of the learning goals for the year were necessarily determined by the curriculum. For example, the goal that students would understand and be able to identify different aspects of culture and their significance came from the curriculum, as did the goal that students could infer character from textual cues. The key for Peter and Judy was how to include the students in designing and pursuing projects that would embed personally interesting ways to meet these goals.

Other learning goals were ones that Judy and Peter articulated based on their professional judgments, their personal knowledge of their students, and their conversation with the teaching profession (such as the goals articulated by state and national standards projects). For example, their goals to help students enter and evoke story worlds or to ask questions and organize information were based on their ongoing knowledge of student needs. One of the goals of the cultural journalism unit, to examine how culture influences choices and the use of technology, had come from the social studies standards.

Most importantly, there were the goals that the students themselves set for their own learning.

Judy tried to incorporate these beliefs into her semester ending portfolio presentations. Early in the semester, she had shown the students a model for an assessment form that they could fill out to report on their learning progress. The idea for the form had come from Kathy Egawa at a workshop on inquiry-based evaluation during the 1995 NCTE Spring Conference in Minneapolis, which Judy had attended. The students contributed their ideas for adapting the form, adding, deleting, and changing items so that the form would reflect their concerns. Judy then created a computer template for the form so that students could continue to amend a personal copy and fill it out. Or if they liked, they could print out the form and complete it by hand. As the end of the semester neared, she discussed the form again with the students, and further changes were made. Students were given some workshop time during the dress-up book report week to complete the form, finalize their portfolios, and prepare for their presentations.

On the form were prompts to help the students describe themselves and their work as readers, writers, and learners. The following prompts were some that particular students chose to describe their reading and learning in their portfolios:

- I am a good reader because:

- Some of the things I do well as I read are:

- One thing I want to get better at as a reader is: and I will try to get better by trying:

- Some favorite books, stories, poems I have read this semester are:

- A reading technique that I like is: because:

- A favorite way of sharing my reading is: because:

- I help others with their reading by:

- When I am reading and have problems, I:

- My best reading work this semester was when:

- I am a good writer because:

- To get started with a piece of writing, I might:

- My favorite writing experience this semester was when:

- When I want to learn something new, I know that I have to:

- I use different kinds of questions for the purposes of:

- I evaluate the questions I ask by:

- The class would be even better for me and my classmates if:

This is just a sampling of the kinds of prompts students generated as a group and selected for use in their individual portfolios.

At the end of the form, there was a page for comments from teachers, group members, friends, and parents.

The completed form itself was a portfolio of observations and reflections. Judy also asked students to pick out three or four of the prompts and to illustrate their learning and improvement with examples of their "best work." The students chose journal entries, written work, SSRs, or other projects that would provide proof of what they knew and could do.

During the presentation, students handed out copies of their completed form to their guests. They then presented illustrations of their work and explained how these examples demonstrated their learning and improvement. The presentations ended with goal setting, applause, and congratulations. The presentations were scheduled in eight-minute blocks before, after, and throughout the school day during the last week of the semester. Judy and Matt together hosted the conferences throughout the week—without him, she could never have done it for 130 students. Even so, it was a stretch. Students not involved as presenters or guests used their class time to free read or to pursue research on their hypermedia project.

Students participate as knowledgeable, reflective, creative, and critical members of a variety of literacy communities.

The goal of the presentations was to assess progress, help the students feel good about how much they had learned, set goals, and emphasize to students that they were part of a supportive learning community that included teachers, group members, friends, and other adults. If parents could not arrange to attend the presentations, as was often the case, a copy of the completed form was sent home. Some parents sent a videotape so that the presentation could be recorded, and Judy was always happy to make those arrangements. She tried to think of the importance of each individual presentation, instead of wondering how she was going to get through 130 of them. The presentations took a lot of time and energy, but Judy thought it was worth it. In the past, she had conducted portfolio interviews privately with students, but she felt that the public presentation and support added an important new dimension to the assessment and made it a kind of formal acknowledgment of the students' hard work and a celebration of it! And what is a life, or a school year, without celebration?

Students conduct research on issues and interests by generating ideas and questions, and by posing problems. They gather, evaluate, and synthesize data from a variety of sources (e.g., print and nonprint texts, artifacts, people) to communicate their discoveries in ways that suit their purpose and audience.

Students participate as knowledgeable, reflective, creative, and critical members of a variety of literacy communities.

Building in Assessment

The cultural journalism project (or "hypermedia project" as they called it privately) started in earnest on the first day of the semester. The checksheets contained a quick "gut check" of the students' standing. Judy revisited the students' Memorable Learning posters that they had created at the beginning of the school year. She reminded them that their job throughout the year, and particularly during this project, was to share their learning with others. She reminded the students of their various audiences for the completed hyperstacks: their group, classmates, third grade reading buddies, partner school, parents, and library users. How could they make their documents a memorable learning experience for others? The students took a look at their posters and identified aspects of memorable learning that could be included in their hyperstack. "Include a game or quiz" was Mike's suggestion. Anticipating one of the books Judy would share as an example format, Krista thought "it would be good to make [the stack] into a kind of tour or trip to the culture—you have to involve the browser somehow." Several students thought it would be important to have good pictures, graphics, maps, and music. "It has to be organized and easy to follow" was Diana's opinion. "People have to be able to get around in [the document]."

HYPERCARD CULTURE CHECKSHEET

1. You have an updated, teacher approved, **plan tree**? ______
2. You have between **5** and **15 cards** with **buttons**?______
(You have a card for each part of your plan tree)
3. Each of your cards has a **title**? ______
4. You have a **table of contents** card?______
5. The **buttons** on your cards take you to a **related card** or back to the table of contents?______
6. Your **map** is related to one of your cards-**not** just a button on your table of contents card?______
7. You have included some **pictures or graphs** on your stack?______
8. You have a **field with a brief summary** on most of your cards?______
9. You have checked your field info for **spelling** and **sentence structure**?__
10. The info in your field has enough detail to be **interesting** and **educational** (someone can learn something **NEW** from it)?______
11. You have **printed out your stacks** and made a **tree** with your cards(1/4 size)?____

Your Name ______________________

Culture ________________

Area ________________

As always with any major project or theme during the year, Peter and Judy tried to provide students with models that they could respond to and rank, which would provide a basis for defining the project and constructing standards for it. The students once again created their own rubric of criteria, and benchmarks for assessing the quality of these included items.

So they started off with each group touring and writing a review of three different hypermedia stacks that were composed over the past two years. As they did so, they discussed ideas they could use in their own stacks, and shortcomings or problems they wanted to avoid.

Students employ a wide range of strategies as they write and use different writing process elements appropriately to communicate with different audiences for a variety of purposes.

Review writing was an important element of the project. When students viewed videotapes or read novels and other major resources featuring information about culture, they composed a review for future students that outlined the kinds of information that could be gleaned and that evaluated the effectiveness of the source. These reviews were composed on a hypercard document they called "Classroom Culture Library." It was just another way of involving the students in creating their own classroom resources. At the end of the project, they reviewed each other's stacks and presentations.

Next day during their combined classes, the students discussed their rankings and evaluations of the stacks, listed criteria, and began to create benchmarks. This student-created rubric was referred to throughout the unit and was amended when necessary. The final form was published and used by the students and teachers during peer editing and assessment. It was stressed to the students throughout the project that assessment would be based on the criteria they had created and agreed to. Some groups wished to amend the rubrics to fit the particular purposes and design of their own stack, and this was allowed.

Some other forms of assessment were also built into the fabric of the project so that self-assessment would be ongoing and would help to inform the process of learning and design.

First, as an entrance ticket to their language arts-social studies block, each student would submit a *daily plan* to one of the teachers, who would quickly check and return it with suggestions. Students then proceeded to the appropriate workstation, whether in the classroom, library, video- and audio-taping area, or computer lab. If students were clearly off-task during the ninety-minute block, they were asked what it was they had agreed to do, and this seemed to keep them highly focused.

For homework, each student kept a *design diary*. At first they kept the diary in their journals, but when the students were ready to design on the computers, they entered this diary into the computer as a separate hypercard. They then made their entries directly on that design diary card for the duration of the project. The design diary was a kind of metacognitive log or reflective journal. At the end of each day, the students related what they had done, reflected on their learning progress, connected it to what they had previously learned, and considered how this latest work would affect their future plans. At this point, students would make a plan for the next day.

The daily plans and self-assessments were fairly quick takes that helped focus students. For example, Troy entered class one day with the following plan: "I will read several Norse myths I have found. Choose one for an SSR. Make notes for my stack." At the end of the period, he wrote: "Learned about Loki the wisdom god who was very important and Thor, the god of thunder. Decided to do story on Thor's stolen hammer for SSR. I think I might do a whole part of my stack on folktales and important characters. Tomorrow I'll read about the stolen hammer again and plan my SSR."

At the end of each week, every student would complete a *self-evaluation*. This evaluation was basically a letter that assessed (1) where the student found herself on her checksheet vis-à-vis the project calendar; (2) how well the student was working with her group, how aware she was of other group members' progress, and how she could be helping the rest of her group; (3) sources of confusions, problems, obstacles, and questions that needed to be addressed; and (4) provided a detailed response to a teacher question about learning, student design or some other feature of the project. These self-evaluations then provided focus for the next week's conferences and the development of minilessons. Judy, Peter, and Matt divided up these evaluations—about forty each—

EVALUATION RUBRIC FOR <u>CULTURE HYPERMEDIA PROJECT</u>
Name_________________________

OUTCOME	17 - 20 POINTS EXCELLENT	1 - 16 POINTS ACCEPTABLE	0 POINTS NOT ACCEPTABLE
Value= 20 points ______ POINTS Multimedia Card Space Justification	Card space has been thoughtfully used and author can justify use of card space.	Author has less than 25% of stack cards that she can not justify space use. Points will be deducted in proportion to number of problem cards for the size of the stack.	Author has 25% or more cards that she can not justify space use.
Value= 20 points ______ POINTS Stack Organization and function	Stack organization follows an easy to use main menu card. The stack organization aids the browser's understanding of the stack's content.	Stack organization follows an easy to use main menu. Stack organization does not get in the way of browser's understanding of content.	Stack does not follow the main menu. Stack organization gets in the way of browser's understanding of content.
Value= 20 points ______ POINTS Information Quality	Text is written in author's own words, is interesting to read, grammatically correct, and properly divided.	Topic is covered well but has problems with grammar, division of information, use of own words, or being boring to read.	Topic coverage has gaps. 25% or more of the cards have problems with text
Value= 20 points ______ POINTS Button Quality	Reasons for all links, button names, icons, and effects are clear and warranted. More than one cross link made in stack or to another stack.	Some mysterious or unjustified links, names, icons, and effects. Points will be deducted in in proportion to the number of problems and the size of the stack. At least one cross link made in stack or to another stack.	Five or more buttons have problems with links, names, icons, or effects. No cross links made in stack or to another stack.
Value=20 points ______ POINTS Audience Involvement	Audience is made to feel involved throughout the stack. Involvement is interesting and maybe even fun.	An attempt has been made to involve the audience. Points awarded depend on effort made throughout the stack.	No observable attempt has been made to involve the audience.
Value= 20 points ______ POINTS Research Quality	Three or more primary and secondary sources have been used and documented. Two of the following have been used: interview, follow-up, or artifact.	Two primary and secondary (myth, story, video etc.) have been used and documented. Along with one interview and one artifact. Points may deducted if information not adequately covered.	Less than two primary and secondary sources, one interview, or one artifact used and documented.

and read them over the weekend, often phoning each other Sunday night to use what they had learned from them and their classroom observations to begin planning out the next week.

This was lesson planning "by the seat of the pants," as Judy called it, and Peter was the most comfortable with it. Though it made her nervous sometimes, she saw how it enabled instruction to fit students' current needs.

The teachers had divided the students into three rotating lists and would try to *conference* with each student on their weekly list two or three times during that week. A few comments would be made on the master list to help out the next responsible team teacher. They would switch lists at the end of each week, and in that way each of the three teachers became familiar with each student's work. It also worked to include Matt as a member of the teaching team in students' eyes, instead of the teacher who worked only with certain students. The students were able to get advice and help from the perspective of different teachers, and the teachers were able to see real progress and to comment upon it during their second or third time around with the students.

A new twist they had planned was to include at least three *round table* discussions during this year's edition of the project. During a round table, students from different groups would get together to share their progress. The first one was for sharing a proposed organization of the stack, the second for sharing some of their completed cards, and the final one for sharing a first draft of their completed stack. The round table group would serve as peer editors as they critiqued and offered suggestions on the work.

As the project began to near completion, students used the rubrics they had agreed upon to continue *self-editing* their own stack and *peer-editing* those of at least two others, and to guide their revision process.

Ultimately, the groups would combine their individual stacks into a group stack, create cross-links between the stacks, and make their *final presentations* to at least three different groups: their social studies class, third grade reading buddies, and during the Parent Open House. There would certainly be feedback from each of these audiences.

Students employ a wide range of strategies as they write and use different writing process elements appropriately to communicate with different audiences for a variety of purposes.

Students participate as knowledgeable, reflective, creative, and critical members of a variety of literacy communities.

Students adjust their use of spoken, written, and visual language (e.g., conventions, style, vocabulary) to communicate effectively with a variety of audiences and for different purposes.

Into Full Swing

Questioning

When the students first brainstormed, categorized, and critiqued each other's questions, their first concerns were whether the questions were researchable and interesting. A lot of students had used the QAR (question-answer relationship) terminology to think about and discuss the questions. The students decided that a research question probably had to be a "Think and Search" question. If it wasn't, it probably was not complex and interesting enough to drive and guide research over the course of eight weeks. A few students thought that a good research question could be "Author and Me," since the researcher had to develop knowledge through interviews, surveys, and other techniques, and since their own personal understanding of the culture was necessary to creating the document. "Right There" questions were probably "OK to help you make one card, but not for a stack," Tony thought. "I mean, it doesn't really seem worth researching–or even like research at all–if you can find the answer in one place. I mean, get real, anybody could do that!"

This growing sense of themselves as researchers who developed knowledge and insight over time was a trend that excited the teaching team. There were also some lively discussions about the place of "On Your Own" questions in a documentary. Would personal opinions have any place in their final product? Why or why not? How were opinions different from the inferences they would be making? What were the costs and benefits to the final stack of including opinions? Some students agreed that opinions did not belong, but some said opinions might be OK to include if they were clearly identified as opinions.

In their gut check, students revisited what they had done so far and set some immediate tasks for the future. At this point, all of the students had successfully completed the criteria for the questioning phase, and all were still involved in the finding information phase of the project. So students conducted their gut check by asking themselves K-W-H questions, a variation of the *K-W-L framework* (Ogle, 1986):

K = What do I already know about my stack topic?
W = What more do I want to know to answer the question about my topic?
H = How might I find more information that will help answer my question?

After asking themselves these questions, the students also asked them of another group member, a classmate not in their group, and an adult. They sent a K-W-H form to their reading buddies to get their feedback as well. Now that

Students adjust their use of spoken, written, and visual language (e.g., conventions, style, vocabulary) to communicate effectively with a variety of audiences and for different purposes.

Students conduct research on issues and interests by generating ideas and questions, and by posing problems. They gather, evaluate, and synthesize data from a variety of sources (e.g., print and nonprint texts, artifacts, people) to communicate their discoveries in ways that suit their purpose and audience.

they knew what their potential audiences knew and wanted to know and had audience suggestions for how to find out, the students were better prepared to begin thinking about how to pursue and present their documentary.

A funny thing about some of the questions was that they seemed driven by student conceptions of schooling instead of their real interests. Mike, for instance, was a bright if somewhat disorganized student. His stack topic was "the economy of Italy," and his question was "How does the free market economy of Italy work?" He had done some reading and had already designated subtopics such as "money system" and "major industries."

During the initial teacher conference, Peter encouraged Mike to survey some other students about what they wanted to know about the Italian economy. His list of their interests included wanting to know what interesting jobs are typically Italian (one girl wanted to know if there were spaghetti makers), how people spent their money, what they did for vacation, how prices for things compared with prices in the United States, and much more. Peter pointed out how these concerns coincided with what his audience had previously listed under "Want to Know."

Mike eventually revised his question to "What are the most interesting jobs in Italian industry?" and he explored topics like designing race cars, the fashion industry, wine tasting, and the influence of the Mafia on industry. Towards the end of the project, he admitted that "this was a lot more fun than what I was going to do."

Judy, Matt, and Peter talked at length about why many students, especially those who were typically successful at school, didn't really exercise the independence that such a project offered them. They seemed to try to fit their project into the mold of what schooling had previously expected of them.

Some students were leading groups interested in studying their own cultural group. Kae was the leader for a group studying Laos. She was already having fun as group members decided on questions about dating rituals, male and female roles, ceremonial dress, and eating habits. Josef was leading a group on Poland, and Maria a group of girls interested in her native Mexico.

These groups seemed in fine shape. Judy was concerned, though, about some of her students like Tim and Curt, who were labeled and sometimes struggled. Could they sustain their enthusiasm for the duration of the project? Would they contribute to and be supported by their group doing Icelandic culture? She hoped they would find enough information about their questions on how entertainment and geological features affected cultural life in Iceland.

Finding and Developing Information

At the end of the previous quarter, Peter had undertaken an intense study of culture with the students. They had compiled lists of questions that anthropologists would ask about aspects of culture, such as communication, education, and entertainment.

Now the focus was on the specific study of self-selected topics about a chosen culture. There were mini-lessons on developing surveys and questionnaires, writing questions, and conducting interviews and on creating video clips, maps, graphs, and other visuals that would help answer their questions. The school had recently purchased one PowerMacintosh with AV capability, and many of the students were eager to use some of its capacities for including video and audio on their hyperstacks.

By the second week of the semester, there was a constant flurry of activity. Informants were visiting the classroom, and different groups were taking field trips to visit other informants, libraries, and museums.

Usually the students interviewed their informant in small groups, but on some occasions the informant would also make a presentation to the whole house. This year a storyteller from East Africa performed his stories for the whole group, and a ranger from a nearby wilderness area gave a slide show about his three-month stay with the Inuits inside the Arctic Circle.

Students develop an understanding of and respect for diversity in language use, patterns, and dialects across cultures, ethnic groups, geographic regions, and social roles.

Some groups were getting together on weekends to watch videos about their culture, listen to music from the culture, or just to discuss and work on their project.

This was a very important phase of the project which the other phases depended on, so the teaching team were real sticklers for making sure the students had found and processed lots of information. Before students organized their information and began designing on the computer, they were expected to have conducted an interview and follow-up questionnaire, to have read a variety of other nonfiction sources (travel books or brochures, history, newspaper and magazine articles) and cultural stories (picture books, myths, folktales), and to have examined nontraditional sources and artifacts (music, videos, clothing, recipes). The teachers expected each student to have a general view of the culture—so that they could help group members and see how their question fit into the whole—and to have specifically pursued their own question.

One or two groups had trouble scheduling interviews until later in the project. This was something they would just have to work around. Some other students found that they couldn't find enough information to answer their question or that they had too much information to include in a stack. The students revisited their work on topics and central focus as mini-lessons were conducted on how to know you had covered a topic and expressed a central focus or point. Then there were mini-lessons on revising topics and questions to make them bigger or smaller. Some of the mini-lessons were conducted with the whole group; others were conducted with only those students who had requested or seemed to need the help.

Curt, for instance, found a whole book on Icelandic waterfalls and another two on volcanic activity in Iceland. He decided, in consultation with his informant, Ragga Jonsdottir, that the volcanoes and geothermal heating of water had more effect on daily life than entertainment. So that became the new topic of his stack.

REFINING A TOPIC

General Topic: Clothing
Make it smaller: 1.summer clothing 1. sandals
2.designer clothing 2.
3.my wardrobe 3.
4.
5.

Make it bigger: 1. 1.

General Topic: African-Americans and Major League Sports

Revised Topic:

General Topic: African-Americans in the military

Revised Topic:

General Topic: General Colin Powell

Make it bigger:

Make it smaller:

For what reasons might you make a topic bigger or smaller?

You should choose a topic about which there is a compelling story to tell. Your topic will control what can be included in the story. It is then your job to find the information necessary to fully understand the topic, clarifying and completing it. Your documentary must represent the topic to your audience so that they understand it. To do so you might have to explain kinds, causes, problems and solutions, stories, examples, etc.

Curt's father was a contractor, and they had both become interested in Icelandic hot baths and heating systems.

Though students were at different points in the project, after three weeks most students seemed to have analyzed a substantial amount of data. At this point, Judy asked each student to choose one of the cultural tales or myths they had read for an SSR performance. This performance should dramatize the story, as always, and dramatize how the student had read and responded to the story. New wrinkles to be included were cutouts for any cultural idea, custom, or motif that the reader noticed in the story, and a cutout for the central focus. After the performance, students were to consider why this story was one that had been traditionally told in this culture.

A few students had not yet found a cultural story, but that was soon remedied. Matt went to a city bookstore and bought two classroom resources for students wanting to read cultural stories. This helped the groups doing Australia and India. The teachers made an intense effort to help any other students who still needed further sources of information. They found that the conferences and the checklists that they initialed really kept kids from falling between the cracks, as in past years. Even Tim, with the help of Ragga, was keeping up. He was busy at work organizing information about the twelve days of Christmas and was going to use a related story for his SSR.

The SSRs were a great success. Judy could see that students were really getting better in how they used the technique to evoke a text and to explore their response to the text and its meaning.

Still, all was not sweetness and light. (When is it?) A couple of parents visited during team meeting time. Their concern: this hypermedia stuff isn't school. What content are our kids learning? The team did their best to justify the unit. "The kids are constructing knowledge and confronting big ideas as they go through this project," Peter told the parents. Judy explained that "the children are confronting big issues that are whole and are meaningful to them. The experience requires students to go through a process of personal learning *and* it serves curricular goals for knowing content—about culture, about stories, about technology, about information sources, and much more. Above all, we want them to know *how* to gain knowledge."

The team was kind of bemused by these questions, but, as Peter said, "If we can't justify why it's good learning, then we shouldn't be doing it."

They also asked each other how they could inform and involve the parents more. How could they meet individual and group concerns? How could they educate the parents about what they were doing? Were P.T.O. meetings or Open Houses ways to do this? Should they be more proactive, or was it enough to write the information letters and react when problems came up? This was a big issue and warranted lots of consideration.

Though most of the students seemed totally into the project, there were a few bellyachers from this camp as well. Most of these complainers were students who had been very successful in school. "Why can't we just do worksheets?" Meg complained. "This is really hard," Eric repeated several times as he analyzed and began organizing his information. He had discovered that he needed to add some information to answer his question and he was feeling sour.

Students use spoken, written, and visual language to accomplish their own purposes (e.g., for learning, enjoyment, persuasion, and the exchange of information).

Judy was reminded of what Rich Lehrer had told them as he had helped them prepare the project: "Don't think that all of the kids are going to thank you for this. After all, you're asking them to take charge of their own learning—and you're asking them to think."

They helped the students as best they could. "Your question is really worth answering," Judy told Eric, and talked him through how he could find the information he needed to add. "You're a real researcher now," Judy told him, "and this is what real researchers do: reframe questions, go back to the data, and work, work, work to understand."

"This project is so big," Mike lamented one day.

"It is, and now you're over the hump," Peter told him. "Soon you'll be doing the fun stuff—designing on the computer and teaching other people about this. You're an expert on it now!"

Mike kind of perked up after that little pep talk and got back to work. The team tried to emphasize that the kids *were* doing something big, that it *was* hard, and therefore they could be proud of their work.

Organizing the Information

The last thing the students had to do before entering the computer lab was to organize their information and complete plan sheets for their first four cards.

There were mini-lessons on using the issue tree to organize the information

CARD PLAN & JUSTIFICATION SHEET

Name ________________ **Hour** _____ **Topic** ______________ **Culture** ____________

Background: I am going to put __________ pattern on this card because... ____________________

Visual: I chose to include ________________ because... ____________________

Link: I linked this card to ______________ because... ____________________

I linked this card to ______________ because... ____________________

I linked this card to ______________ because... ____________________

Icon: I used a ____________ icon because... ____________________

I used a ____________ icon because... ____________________

I used a ____________ icon because... ____________________

Effect: I used ____________ effect because... ____________________

I used ____________ effect because... ____________________

I used ____________ effect because... ____________________

Grammar: The spelling in my text field is correct. ________

The sentence structure in my text field is correct. ______

Content: The content of my text field is meaningful to my topic and interesting to read. ______

into categories and details. There was a mini-lesson on translating the issue tree into an organization of particular cards, and the students discussed what kinds of information could go together on a single card.

On the basis of this work, students used index cards to designate the topic of each card they proposed to put into their stack. They used string to show the connections between cards. This was critiqued in round tables, and the issue trees were then revised.

Finally, group members reviewed and combined their issue trees into a giant tree. They then provided cross-links within and between their trees to make a web. In this way, students were familiarizing themselves once again with each other's work and considering how their individual stacks would work together to illuminate both their individual questions and their general cultural topic.

The students completed card plan sheets as they designed their initial cards. The plan sheets were designed to help students consider all of the elements needed on a card and how the card worked within the stack. Once students had completed three or four successful plan sheets, they were free to design cards without the sheets.

Being There

The first two days that the lab was available, students were trickling in to the computer room. But after that, most of them had completed the organization phase and card planning, and the computer lab bustled with activity from daybreak until the students were chased out at 4 p.m.

Because there were only twenty-eight computers, the team decided to break the students out of the combined class schedule so that they reported to separate language arts and social studies classes. During social studies, each student would have forty-five minutes on a computer. If they weren't quite ready for designing, they would work with Matt in the library. In language arts, Judy was going to address some issues that the team had noticed in the first few cards the students had designed.

First, there was the problem of plagiarism. Judy found and copied three articles from current magazines about plagiarism cases. She asked the students to read the articles and answer these three questions: What is plagiarism? Why do people plagiarize? How can it be avoided?

Students adjust their use of spoken, written, and visual language (e.g., conventions, style, vocabulary) to communicate effectively with a variety of audiences and for different purposes.

After a classroom discussion of the issue, Judy provided the students with a paragraph from one of the articles they had just read and with fifteen examples of sentences that quoted or paraphrased information from the article. The students identified the sentences that correctly used quotation marks or a citation (the class was using APA style) to avoid plagiarism, and they corrected those versions that were examples of plagiarism.

Students apply knowledge of language structure, language conventions (e.g., spelling and punctuation), media techniques, figurative language, and genre to create, critique, and discuss print and nonprint texts.

Another problem was that many students were trying to describe important cultural settings or events, but felt that their cards were "boring." So Judy planned out a sequence of lessons on descriptive, sensory writing.

First, they looked at some of the actual cards that students had made but found dissatisfying. The class discussed what would make a description interesting and exciting to read and made a quick rubric. They then chose a short example text from one of the cards that they agreed to rewrite for a contest to be played two days later.

On the next day, Judy guided students through a sequence of assignments for making writing more specific and sensory. First, students rewrote headlines to make them more zippy and specific. Then the fun started as they rewrote the school cafeteria menu to make the food sound wonderfully enticing—and then again to make it sound disgusting. Judy also introduced the students to a description of a planned retirement community—with all of the adjectives deleted. The students added their own adjectives and discussed the resulting feeling and tone of the piece. The class then brainstormed ideas for using the senses, such as sound devices and metaphors, that would really help a reader to experience a place. The students were to use these ideas as they revised the chosen card for tomorrow's contest.

On game day, they played the *Revision Playoff.* The class divided in half and gave their revised place descriptions (identified only with an alias or phone number so that no one would know the writer) to the other side of the classroom. Each side divided into three smaller groups that read two descriptions at a time, and then decided from this head-to-head combat which one was best. They wrote Praise, Question, and Polish comments on each paper. The winning description was then forwarded to the teacher to continue on in the playoff. (There was also a loser's bracket so that each paper would be read twice.) In turn, the winning entry was read against another winning description. Eventually, each side of the classroom produced a description they thought was best when measured against the rubric devised two days earlier. The winners from each side were read aloud and discussed, and a grand champion was crowned! The class ended with a discussion of descriptive techniques that helped readers feel like they were there in the scene, experiencing a significant setting or event.

The next day, on a whim, Judy brought in some journal entries from the poet James Wright and showed how his descriptions had been boiled down into poems. What details were most important to experiencing a place? What details had the poet chosen? What had he deleted and added? Why? Judy challenged the students to use a place description from their journals to write their own *boil-down poem.* They also discussed how poetry could be used to present information or cultural perspectives as part of their documentaries.

Judy was pleased with the lesson sequence. It had taken three class days, addressed a problem students were having, and had been a lot of fun for them.

Students read a wide range of print and nonprint texts to build an understanding of texts, of themselves, and of the cultures of the United States and the world; to acquire new information; to respond to the needs and demands of society and the workplace; and for personal fulfillment. Among these texts are fiction and nonfiction, classic and contemporary works.

Students conduct research on issues and interests by generating ideas and questions, and by posing problems. They gather, evaluate, and synthesize data from a variety of sources (e.g., print and nonprint texts, artifacts, people) to communicate their discoveries in ways that suit their purpose and audience.

Students as Designers

After a week, Judy took her language arts classes to the computer lab for computer time, and Peter taught mini-lessons during the scheduled social studies class.

By now, many students had completed their basic cards and information fields and were beginning to add in design features such as backgrounds, specialized icons for buttons, graphics, and animation.

"As exciting as the computer tools are for the kids," Peter said one day, "we could be doing this whole project without the computer technology."

"You mean by having them create books or museum exhibits for each other?"

"Yeah, and there are other possibilities too. What we're doing is good learning. You don't need computers for that. Like Picasso said: 'Computers are useless; they don't ask questions.'"

"Why are we using them then?" Judy asked. "Why don't we do the project next year without the computers? It would solve some problems, like the way we tie up the lab, the computers going down, kids losing their disks . . ."

Students use a variety of technological and informational resources (e.g., libraries, databases, computer networks, video) to gather and synthesize information and to create and communicate knowledge.

"We live in a technological world, Jude," Peter said. "The kids find the computer motivating, and they're learning how to use the possibilities of technology for their own purposes. In the future, a kid who doesn't know how to read and write on hypermedia will be a kind of illiterate. And it extends their abilities. The products look great and they take pride in them. I was just wishing we could get the kids online so they could do research on the World Wide Web, do e-mail with their informants and our partner school, stuff like that."

"So," Judy joked, "even though we don't need technology to do student-designed and student-centered learning, we'll use more of it next year anyway?"

Peter laughed and ducked into his classroom.

Students develop an understanding of and respect for diversity in language use, patterns, and dialects across cultures, ethnic groups, geographic regions, and social roles.

Students participate as knowledgeable, reflective, creative, and critical members of a variety of literacy communities.

Judy was delighted to see how the kids were developing expertise in several different dimensions of the project. Nicky, for instance, was great at asking questions, and Mike—bless his heart!—had become excellent at critiquing issue trees. They served as resident gurus for other students.

The kids were also becoming experts on their particular culture and cultural questions and could often be heard in class or in the lunchroom discussing what they had learned and comparing it with other cultures that were being studied or with the students' growing awareness of their own culture.

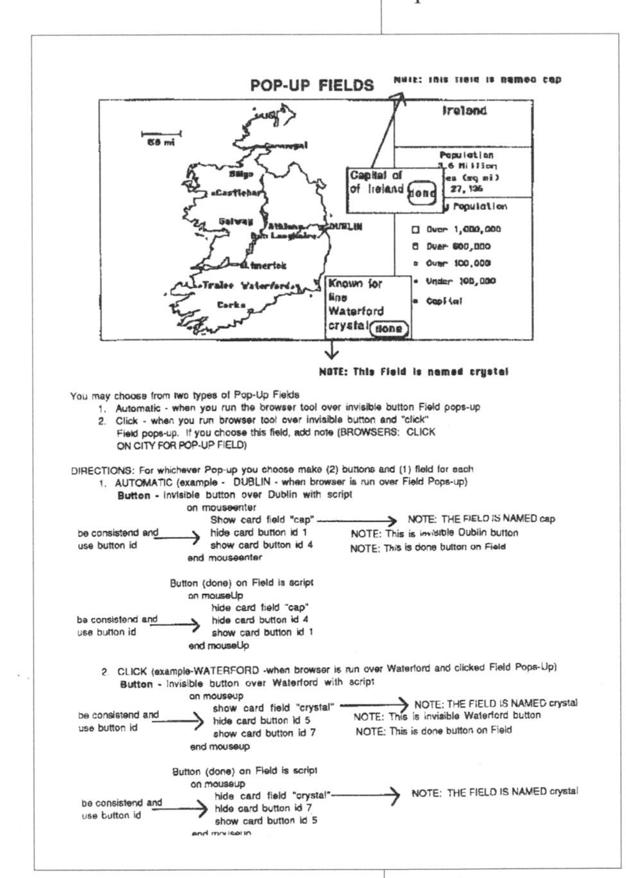

POP-UP FIELDS

You may choose from two types of Pop-Up Fields

1. Automatic - when you run the browser tool over invisible button Field pops-up
2. Click - when you run browser tool over invisible button and "click" Field pops-up. If you choose this field, add note (BROWSERS: CLICK ON CITY FOR POP-UP FIELD)

DIRECTIONS: For whichever Pop-up you choose make (2) buttons and (1) field for each

1. AUTOMATIC (example - DUBLIN - when browser is run over Field Pops-up)
Button - Invisible button over Dublin with script

```
on mouseenter
    Show card field "cap"  ——> NOTE: THE FIELD IS NAMED cap
    hide card button id 1      NOTE: This is invisible Dublin button
    show card button id 4      NOTE: This is done button on Field
end mouseenter
```

(be consistend and use button id)

Button (done) on Field is script

```
on mouseUp
    hide card field "cap"
    hide card button id 4
    show card button id 1
end mouseUp
```

(be consistend and use button id)

2. CLICK (example-WATERFORD -when browser is run over Waterford and clicked Field Pops-Up)
Button - Invisible button over Waterford with script

```
on mouseup
    show card field "crystal"  ——> NOTE: THE FIELD IS NAMED crystal
    hide card button id 5          NOTE: This is invisible Waterford button
    show card button id 7          NOTE: This is done button on Field
end mouseup
```

(be consistend and use button id)

Button (done) on Field is script

```
on mouseup
    hide card field "crystal"  ——> NOTE: THE FIELD IS NAMED crystal
    hide card button id 7
    show card button id 5
end mouseup
```

(be consistend and use button id)

Most striking were the students who were becoming hypermedia experts. They were usually students who were labeled or who had not typically been successful in school. Tony figured out on his own how to do flip card animations, and with Tim and the HyperCard book had figured out how to do drag animation. They were now involved in helping other students learn this technique as well. Stephanie figured out how to create pop-up fields and worked with Peter to make a help sheet for other students who wanted to try making one.

"These kids are something," Matt told Judy, "but it's not learning disabled. Look at how Tim is teaching kids drag animation! When they get the chance to work with tools like hypermedia, you can see how they work and solve problems. Maybe it's more like they have an allergy to normal school."

In fact, when a computer problem or question arose, the team would usually call out: "Who knows how to do pop-up fields?" or "How do you get off of a background?" And the kids would end up helping each other. Many had far outstripped the teachers' knowledge of hypermedia, and the team was constantly learning from the kids about the possibilities of the program.

As exciting as this was, a lot of the students were using flashy effects that did not contribute to the meaning or point of their stack. The team was constantly asking students to justify the effects they created in terms of their larger purposes.

Jon, for example, was working on the topic of travel and transportation in Norway. He created a drag animation of a bus crashing over a cliff to jazz up one of his cards. Why? "It looks cool. It'll catch attention!" Were there a lot of bus accidents in Norway? This sent Jon back to the library to find out about the road safety record in Norway. He found it was excellent. Wanting to keep the animation, he labeled the card: "Something you won't see in Norway," and he added a textual field outlining the safety record of Norwegian road travel. And when a peer editor pointed out that he had made a speed limit sign with miles per hour, Jon looked up road signs from Europe and changed both the shape of the sign and pointed out that the speed limit was now calculated in kilometers.

Classroom Critiques

Judy had to admit that she was getting pretty exhausted. Some afternoons she could almost feel her hair graying and her liver quivering from the intensity of the day. She looked forward to reading a book with her students and leaving the computer room behind. But as exhausted as she was, she knew the students were engaged with their learning. Students filled the lab throughout the day, and many were continuing to do research for information they wanted to add. Some students were far enough ahead with their project that they were finishing up the design of their stack and were pursuing free reading for homework. A few students had formed book clubs and were already thinking about their final project, to be pursued during the spring quarter.

Students use spoken, written, and visual language to accomplish their own purposes (e.g., for learning, enjoyment, persuasion, and the exchange of information).

As they neared the end of the project, it was time to print out some of the finished cards and have round table critique sessions. Every student brought printouts of two finished cards to the round table. Judy had made overheads of a couple of cards, and the group worked together to model positive critiques.

"As I walk around, what kind of things should I be hearing?" she asked the class, and recorded their list on the board. "What kind of things should I not be hearing?"

For the round tables and peer editing, the students used the *P-Q-P technique*. First, there would be Praise for the product, then Questions, and finally suggestions for Polishing it.

As was usual, the class modeled the process as a whole class with a card Monica had agreed could be used on the topic of "Mayday in Germany" from her stack on the question: "How are holidays important to the Germans?" The class started by praising Monica for creating her own graphic of a Maypole. The card fit her topic and question. It was interesting that Germans drank scented wine and woodruff ice and that the strawberries in Germany were different from ours. They liked the icon she had made herself for the button connecting this card to one about Easter.

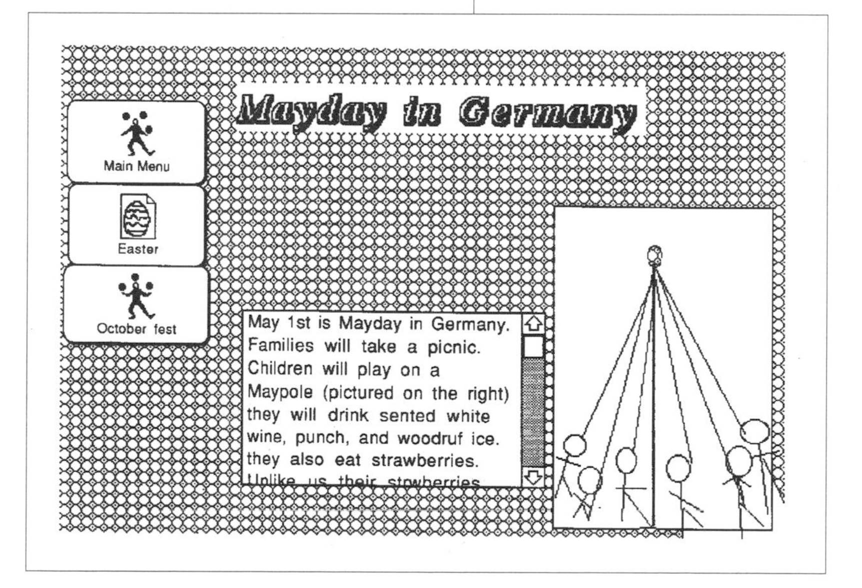

The class had a lot of questions too. Rod wanted to know why the icons on two buttons were the same. "How does that help me understand where I'm going [when I push the button]?" he asked. "If I'm not going to the same place why is there the same picture?"

Why didn't she make her field bigger instead of scrolling it? After all, she had room. Mike felt that she "could use her space better. Fill up the background with what she's got instead of hiding it [in a scroll]."

What was scented wine? How was it scented? What game do you play on a Maypole? What's woodruff ice? What's the purpose of this holiday anyway?

A lot of the questions had included suggestions for polishing, but there were still a few more. What is May Day called in Germany? And there was a lot of laughter as Jon suggested the graphic be changed so that some of the people don't look "like they are hanging from their necks or something!" Monica laughed too, but Judy reminded the students to be considerate of each other during the critiques and not say anything that would be hurtful to someone else, "especially considering all of the hard work we've all been doing. We're trying to help each other, not criticize."

Students adjust their use of spoken, written, and visual language (e.g., conventions, style, vocabulary) to communicate effectively with a variety of audiences and for different purposes.

Students participate as knowledgeable, reflective, creative, and critical members of a variety of literacy communities.

In fact, this week's weekly self-evaluation question was about what they now felt was expected of someone who worked positively in a group and how they were working to meet those expectations.

Revision

The schedule for presentations was set throughout the next week. On Tuesday there would be class presentations, then their third grade reading buddies would be coming to the middle school for a visit on Thursday. On Thursday evening they would show the museum exhibits and offer hypermedia demonstrations during an Open House for the parents and community. The Open House was part of a larger school learning fair, so many people besides parents would be visiting their demonstrations. The students were busily working on revising cards and creating new button links between cards, trying to make their stacks more interesting and informative for their audience. Mini-lessons and peer editing for correct sentences and spelling continued apace to the mantra "People are going to read this!"

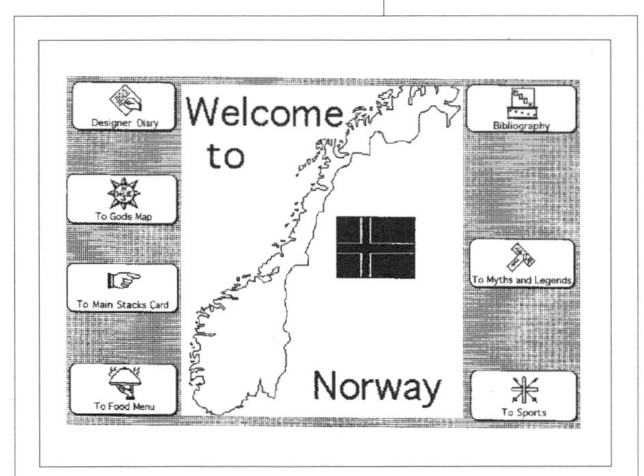

Judy and Peter had challenged the groups to come up with some way to assess what the audience learned from their stacks. As a result, some groups were writing interview questions. Several groups and some individual students were creating interactive hypercard quizzes and game show cards at the end of their stack to evaluate what the browser had learned. Anna and Nicky, upon finishing a quiz card with sound effects, told Judy that "we could have spent the whole year on this [hypermedia project]." Judy was glad they felt that way.

Still, it seemed that a teacher's—and a learner's—greatest commodity was her time and energy. One had to decide how to spend it, and eight weeks would have been spent creating these documents when the presentations were done. It had been a challenging and satisfying experience filled with a lot of various learning activities. For Judy (and for some of her students, she guessed) it was time to celebrate and move on.

Presenting What We Know: Looking to the Future

The presentations went well, and the kids were proud of their work. The reading buddies and the public had been fascinated by the displays and the documents. Some students wound down the Open House by teaching a group from the senior citizen center how to create hypercards.

The local newspaper ran a spread with a description of the project, photos of students presenting their work, and a request from Peter, Matt, and Judy for community volunteers who would like to help out with the project next year.

Just as they were congratulating themselves, they were called into the office. The principal wanted to inform them of a complaint from the high school that "hypermedia isn't part of the language arts or social studies curriculum."

Peter threw his hands up. "It's *not* the curriculum. The project is how we're creating and delivering the curriculum with our students!"

"I know," the principal said, "but I wanted to keep you informed. They're concerned about whether you're addressing some other issues if you are spending so much time on this."

"Well," Peter observed as they left the office, "this highlights the difference between middle school's emphases on the student and learning processes and the high school's emphasis on content area knowledge."

"But you can't have one without the other," Judy argued. "The students couldn't have learned anything from this project if they hadn't learned some information to think with and manipulate. They learned information *and* they learned how to use it, think with it, express it. I think it's just an issue of who decides what gets learned. Some teachers decide for the students. We're trying to find a space for students to make some of their own choices."

"I think what we need to do," Matt offered, "is to just keep conversing with people. Make it clear that we're just struggling, like everybody else, to find the best way to work with our incredibly diverse population. Tell them what evidence we have that this works. Not isolate ourselves from them but remain part of the conversation."

"Maybe we need to do more conversing with the high school people. Why don't we invite them to the Open House next year? And what about our own middle school colleagues? Maybe we should be working and conversing more with them?" Judy asked.

Once back in Peter's classroom, they talked awhile about choice: How much choice should students be given? When should teachers intervene? Is there information every student needs to know? What is it and how can it best be taught? How could they improve this project for next year? How could they do more to connect the study of culture more closely to a look at culture in the students' own lives? They agreed that Kae, Josef, and Maria had done a lot to help their groups see what it was like to be an immigrant and what happened when culture merged with culture. But what about the other groups?

Like nearly all discussions that they had, this one ended with a practical question: What should we do next?

"Time. It's such a problem. There's so much that could be done and so little time," Matt mused.

"That's why we have to make sure the kids are interested and totally engaged in what we do decide to do together–that it's vital and useful to them and looks to the future," Peter insisted.

"Since we can't do everything," Judy threw in, "we and all of the students need to constantly ask, 'Why did we include this?' 'What good is it?' 'What does this learning communicate, how does it help us understand and grow?'"

"Whatever direction we take now," Peter said, "I want the kids to be making things of value to them, opening doors to reshape the future, start taking on the responsibilities of citizenship. But how?"

The team had planned the year to move from personal concerns to concerns about the world, from "Who am I?" to "What is my place in the world?" Peter had units on social change and citizenship that he was still supposed to cover. Judy was supposed to cover an array of skills on reading and writing flexibly from multiple perspectives and for various purposes. They felt that they had already addressed a lot of these issues, but that a good final project would specifically embed all of these concerns. Matt, pleased with how the labeled students in his charge had risen to the challenge of the cultural journalism-hypermedia project, was throwing his lot in again with Peter and Judy, instead of doing pull-out work.

"Let's tell the students what curricular issues we have yet to cover and see what they think we should do," Peter suggested. "Ask them, à la the Foxfire approach, how we could best cover it."

"I think we should ask them what kind of world they want to live in and how they could help to make the world more that way. That would cover social change and citizenship," thought Judy.

"Questions beget questions," Matt observed. "I wonder what they'll come up with?"

"Maybe there could be some kind of community service component," said Peter. "We could brainstorm about that with the kids."

"It's the kids' lives–who they are and what they could be–that is really the curriculum," said Matt. "Anything else is going to get lost."

Judy joined in with, "This is what we need to be asking: How should schools help us live out our values? How can schools be a place for becoming and growing? How can we work together to build personal and social responsibility? Maybe the big understanding we should try to pursue in this next unit would be understanding social issues and how to work for social justice."

"Teaching can certainly be an adventure, if you let it. And if you think it through, maybe you can still throw some meaty bones to the curriculum watchdogs," Matt offered, and the three of them laughed.

Some Standards Highlighted

Meaning: Students work with a variety of cultural resources and informants to explore and express understandings regarding their own research questions. They work to understand how culture fulfills group needs and expresses group values.

Fluency and control: Students use a variety of strategies to pursue their own research: select topics, ask questions, find and develop information, analyze and organize information, add to it, design representations of the information, reflect, edit, and present findings. Throughout, students blend reading, writing, speaking, listening, and media activities into their work.

Critical analysis: Students create and present personal portfolios to assess their own learning. Students critique each other's research questions and plan their trees, research, final documents, and presentations. Students build their own critical standards and rubric for the project and then apply these standards to their own work and that of their classmates.

Knowledge acquisition: Students learn about cultural questions of their choice and use the completed hypermedia documents to teach each other. Students learn how to learn.

Creativity: Students use hypermedia tools to communicate meanings through a variety of media. Students use symbolic story representations to share cultural stories.

Cultural diversity: Students study a variety of primary and secondary cultural resources and work with a cultural informant to pursue understanding of a culture.

Second language: Students make use of cultural terms and the language of the culture in their stacks. Some students include glossaries or cultural dictionaries.

Language diversity: Through their informants, students learn about the linguistic diversity of various cultural groups living in the United States.

Resources

Student-Designed Learning on Hypermedia

Albright [Erickson], J. (1992). *Analysis of discourse in a hypermedia design environment.* Unpublished master's thesis. University of Wisconsin–Madison.

Bolter, J. D. (1991). *The writing space: The computer, hypertext, and the history of writing.* Hillsdale, NJ: Erlbaum.

Carver, S., Lehrer, R., Connell, T., & Erickson, J. (1992). Learning by hypermedia design: Issues of assessment and implementation. *Educational Psychologist, 27* (3), 385–404.

diSessa, A. (1992). Images of learning. In E. DeCorte, M. Linn, H. Mandl, & L. Verschaffel (Eds.). *Computer-based learning environments and problem-solving.* NATO series ASI series F, pp. 19–40. New York: Springer-Verlag.

Engst, A. C. (1994). *Internet starter kit for Macintosh* (2nd ed.). Indianapolis: Hayden Books.

Harris, J. (1994). *Way of the ferret: Finding educational resources on the Internet.* Eugene, OR: International Society for Technology in Education.

Lehrer, R., Erickson, J., & Connell, T. (1994). Learning by designing hypermedia documents. *Computers in the Schools, 10* (1/2), 227–254.

Muir, M. (In press). *Kindling the fire: A classroom guide to curriculum based hypercard projects.* Eugene, OR: International Society for Technology in Education.

Perkins, D. N. (1986). *Knowledge as design.* Hillsdale, NJ: Erlbaum.

Effective Middle School Curriculum Design

Arnold, J. (1990). *Visions of teaching and learning: Eighty exemplary middle level projects.* Columbus, OH: National Middle School Association.

Arnold, J. (1993). A curriculum to empower young adolescents. *Midpoints, 4* (1) 1–11. Columbus, OH: National Middle School Association.

Beane, J. (1993). *A middle school curriculum: From rhetoric to reality.* (2nd ed.). Columbus, OH: National Middle School Association.

Brazee, E., & Capelluti, J. (1993, November). Why an integrative curriculum is needed for the middle level: A recent rationale. *NELMS Journal,*12–22. New England League of Middle Schools.

Brazee, E., & Capelluti, J. (1995). *Dissolving boundaries: Toward an integrated curriculum.* Columbus, OH: National Middle School Association.

George, P., Stevenson, C., Thomason, J., & Beane, J. (1992). *The middle school–and beyond.* Alexandria, VA: Association for Supervision and Curriculum Development.

McDonogh, L. (1991, November). Middle level curriculum: The search for self and social meaning. *Middle School Journal.* Columbus, OH: National Middle School Association.

Siu-Runyan, Y., & Faircloth, C. V. (Eds.). (1995). *Beyond separate subjects: Integrative learning at the middle level.* Norwood, MA: Christopher Gordon.

Stevenson, C., & Carr, J. (1993). *Integrated studies in the middle grades: Dancing through walls.* New York: Teachers College Press.

Swaim, S., et al. (1992). *Middle level curriculum: A work in progress. The initial position paper of the National Middle School Association.* Columbus, OH: National Middle School Association.

Van Hoose, J., & Strahan, D. (1988). *Young adolescent development and school practices: Promoting harmony.* Columbus, OH: National Middle School Association.

Multiculturalism and the Language Arts

Banks, J. A. (1991). *Teaching strategies for ethnic studies* (5th ed.). Boston: Allyn & Bacon.

Banks, J. A. (1991/1992). Multicultural education: For freedom's sake. *Educational Leadership, 49,* 32–36.

Banks, J. A. (1993). The canon debate, knowledge construction, and multicultural education. *Educational Researcher, 22* (5), 4–14.

Banks, J. A., & Banks, C. A. (1989). *Multicultural education: Issues and perspectives.* Boston: Allyn & Bacon.

Leinwand, G. (Comp.). (1971). *Minorities all.* New York: Washington Square Press.

Smagorinsky, P. (1992). Towards a civic education in a multicultural society: Ethical problems in teaching literature. *English Education, 24* (4), 212–228.

Spears-Bunton, L. A. (1990). Welcome to my house: African American and European American students' responses to Virginia Hamilton's *House of Dies Drear. Journal of Negro Education, 59* (4), 566–576.

Stotsky, S. (1995). Guidelines for selecting European ethnic literature for interdisciplinary courses. *English Leadership Quarterly, 17* (1), 1–6.

Wheeler, T. C. (Ed.). (1971). *The immigrant experience: The anguish of becoming American.* New York: Dial Press.

Chapter Five

Putting It All Together

The Shape of the Curriculum

When Judy and Peter had begun to change their teaching several years ago, integrating instruction and working towards large-scale student-designed projects, they had been concerned about creating a coherent curriculum with their students. They wanted the curriculum they created to begin with students' prior knowledge and interest and to build on these in rigorous and challenging ways. They didn't want to be pariahs; though they had been given the freedom to create this kind of curriculum when the junior high had become a middle school, they wanted to make an effort to cover curricular content and skills that the district had designated as important. They didn't want to set themselves outside the pale; they merely wanted to embed these skills and content in vital and holistic learning experiences.

Although there was freedom, it was difficult and politically tricky to make use of it. They had found that they constantly had to justify this new curriculum to students, parents, colleagues, and themselves. That wasn't bad, when you could engage in conversation. It was important to have thought through your purposes and the methods of reaching them and to be able to justify these. But some people had the attitude that "different is wrong" and you couldn't engage in conversation with people who weren't willing to listen and exchange with you. Still, what could you do but keep trying to communicate and give it your best?

When Judy and Peter had outlined a year of critical learning experiences that would accommodate student choice, they had conceived of it as a movement from order to adventure; from routine teaching to teaching that was more individual, spontaneous, complex, and open-ended; from units with some set content and assignments to units that were empty forms that could be filled by concerns and activities that were negotiated with students. They wanted the year and the units that made up the year to move from the concrete to the abstract, from stories to a consideration of what and how stories mean, from knowledge to action, from the self to the world. Within this process, they wanted to stretch their students, continually upping the ante and asking for elaborations.

The progression might have been rough and uneven, but it had informed their purposes and planning. Teaching, Judy and Peter had decided, was a messy and complex and intensely human business. It was about enabling the choices and supporting the learning of others. They tried to provide more structured and scaffolded experiences early in the year as students were learning new tools and skills. Later, the students were asked to extend their use of these tools in more independent and complex situations.

This kind of learning *was* messy and sometimes loud. One day the custodian had told Judy that he could identify good teachers because, when he passed their classrooms, "it's total quiet," and when he cleaned their rooms, "the desks are in rows and there's no paper and other crap all over the floor like it was a cow barn." Judy knew this was a complaint about her own teaching, and especially about the state of the classroom after students had been creating symbolic story representations (SSRs) or filming video shows.

Teaching, Judy liked to say, was an "act of faith in the future." For her, creating a vision of what students could do and be, helping them to set high standards and to strive towards them, was an ethical venture and imperative that expressed that faith.

The year had also been framed by the team's shared philosophy of learning, which they often discussed amongst themselves and with others. Above all, they believed that students had to use their prior knowledge and personal interests to build bridges to new understandings. They believed that understandings had to be constructed through the hands-on activities of the learners. They had struggled with how to implement a constructivist notion of the classroom, and they had settled on the idea of "design"as the best way to do so—for them, anyway, and at this time. This model provided an approach that was both "learner centered" and "teacher guided" (Dewey, 1910).

Such teaching was certainly adventurous. They had been helped in their thinking about design by Perkins (1986), who argued that when learning is recast as a process of design, then students experience knowledge as a human construction situated in time and place and informed by purpose and function. Knowledge gained through design was continually transformed by new needs, information, and perspectives and considered real audiences.

Everything they had pursued this year, whether in their own classrooms or through integrated units—the profile project and psychology stack, the SSRs, the dramas, the cultural journalism projects, the presentations—everything had been informed by the model of design. This in turn had transformed their role as teachers from "the sage on the stage" transmitting information to "the guide on the ride," a facilitator and coach learning and creating knowledge along with the students. Student-designed learning meant giving over responsibility to students, a balance of individual and small-group work, individualized instruction, mini-lessons at the point of need, and public sharing of what had been learned. Created knowledge, they had learned from their students, was something that demanded to be shared.

So what kinds of skills and processes were necessary to creating, designing, and sharing knowledge? These were the big procedural things that Judy and Peter had worked on during the year in the context of the learning projects. Judy had tried to keep her list short, consistent with her desire to "do less to do more."

Students read a wide range of print and nonprint texts to build an understanding of texts, of themselves, and of the cultures of the United States and the world; to acquire new information; to respond to the needs and demands of society and the workplace; and for personal fulfillment. Among these texts are fiction and nonfiction, classic and contemporary works.

Students apply a wide range of strategies to comprehend, interpret, evaluate, and appreciate texts. They draw on their prior experience, their interactions with other readers and writers, their knowledge of word meaning and other texts, their word identification strategies, and their understanding of textual features (e.g., sound-letter correspondence, sentence structure, context, graphics).

Students employ a wide range of strategies as they write and use different writing process elements appropriately to communicate with different audiences for a variety of purposes.

Students apply knowledge of language structure, language conventions (e.g., spelling and punctuation), media techniques, figurative language, and genre to create, critique, and discuss print and nonprint texts.

Students use spoken, written, and visual language to accomplish their own purposes (e.g., for learning, enjoyment, persuasion, and the exchange of information).

Students conduct research on issues and interests by generating ideas and questions, and by posing problems. They gather, evaluate, and synthesize data from a variety of sources (e.g., print and nonprint texts, artifacts, people) to communicate their discoveries in ways that suit their purpose and audience.

First, she wanted her students to construct an active role for themselves as readers to evoke, visualize, empathize, connect, and reflect their way through rich textual experiences. This meant that they would bring their own questions to texts and use a repertoire of meaning-making strategies with awareness. She wanted them to read a variety of texts, including their own and those of classmates, and to respond to these texts through a variety of means: writing, drama, art, discussion.

Secondly, she wanted students to compose a variety of texts (primarily written, but also dramatic, visual, musical) to make sense of the world for a variety of audiences and purposes. Grammar and usage had always been a sticky issue for Judy. She had decided to address correct usage in the context of student writing and its needs. That meant focusing on big issues such as sentence correctness, inflection, and tense that she knew were problems for this age group, or on needs that became apparent as students pursued their own writing.

She wanted students to read and compose for their own purposes and to select their own materials and topics. Judy's brother liked to tell what he called a riddle: What makes you happier, helps you live longer, and keeps you out of jail? The answer was to read for personal pleasure at least fifteen minutes a day. He claimed he had the research to back it up! Judy believed it, based solely on her personal experience. Above all, she wanted her students to see reading and learning as personally powerful and joyous pursuits.

Throughout the year, she wanted the students to be learning how to learn: asking personally significant questions; finding and developing information; analyzing, adding, and organizing the information; representing, sharing, and revising what had been learned. She wanted them to make informed judgments, take positions, reflect on and develop critical standards for their learning, and act upon what they had learned in socially responsible ways. She also wanted students to consider how language helped them to learn and to consider the relationships between language and thought, language and culture, language and other means of expression.

Maybe this was still too much, but these were the general themes that were the piston rods in the engine of her current thinking about teaching. She felt that the design model was a good way to serve those themes.

Although Judy's emphasis was on learning to learn, she did want students to learn content knowledge too. Knowledge of stories and relationships became tools to think with. This final quarter, the team decided that they would teach content about social issues and civil rights and how one can work for social change in the United States. They wanted students to understand the nature and causes of social issues and some history of how these issues had been and could be best addressed.

The Space Traders

The team decided to work in their separate classrooms for five or six weeks. Matt would join those class periods with the most mainstreamed students, so at times he would be working with both Judy and Peter. The team would do some reading with their students and work with them to identify important social issues, brainstorm a related research or service project that could be pursued and reported on, and help groups get started. The last four or five weeks of the year, they would go back to working in combined classes that would basically be workshop time for the students to pursue their integrated curriculum projects.

Because submissions were due for the school literary magazine, some students requested to do some more work on poetry. Judy spent three days with the students writing poems after the models of Emily Dickinson, Wallace Stevens, and Gary Snyder. They talked about metaphor, abstract and concrete language, comparison and contrast, evocative detail, and much more as they composed and shared their poems. Then each student went back through the poems written during the year and spent a day formatting and illustrating a poetry page for a class anthology. Those students who had a poem or another piece of writing for the literary magazine were encouraged to submit it.

Judy had talked with her students during this week about doing another drama to set up the final unit, and they had readily agreed. This drama would be different from the story drama they had pursued earlier in the year. This would be a "process drama" that was suggested by a text, but that the students would play out in their own way. Though Judy would try to structure the drama to help students consider and be challenged by social concerns and issues, the group would basically determine the shape of the drama through their own questions and responses to the dramatic situations.

In consultation with her friend, drama educator Brian Edmiston, Judy decided to base the drama on an idea of Derek Bell's from his story "The Space Traders." In this story, the America of the twenty-first century is bankrupt and in disrepair when a fleet of space traders arrive on the scene. They offer to exchange gold to prop up the economy, chemicals to clean the environment, processes for repairing the infrastructure, and much more. In return, they want only to be able to take with them all citizens of African descent. Judy and Brian decided to make one change; in their drama the aliens would ask for that subgroup of people least valued by the general culture. This would give the students the freedom to designate that group for themselves, and then would require them to examine the reasons or prejudices that had led to that choice.

Brian came in and helped to structure the drama. As always, Judy felt that anything anyone could do to help teach the children made everyone's life richer. This was certainly the case with Brian, and he was welcomed into the classroom by everyone.

On the first day, there was a brief review of the responsibilities of government and its relationship to the citizenry. Since Peter had just begun his unit on citizenship, the students jumped in quickly with their answers. Brian announced that in the drama world America was suffering great problems, and he outlined these. He asked the students in what role they would feel most capable of addressing these problems. All classes chose to assume the roles of senators or other legislators.

Once in the drama world, the senators were asked to list all of the items supported by the current budget: What problems, issues, programs, and people did the government spend money on? Subcommittees of three or four students made their lists and then reported to the floor. Judy recorded all of the student responses on the board. As a group, they then classified their list into

Students read a wide range of print and nonprint texts to build an understanding of texts, of themselves, and of the cultures of the United States and the world; to acquire new information; to respond to the needs and demands of society and the workplace; and for personal fulfillment. Among these texts are fiction and nonfiction, classic and contemporary works.

Students apply knowledge of language structure, language conventions (e.g., spelling and punctuation), media techniques, figurative language, and genre to create, critique, and discuss print and nonprint texts.

Students conduct research on issues and interests by generating ideas and questions, and by posing problems. They gather, evaluate, and synthesize data from a variety of sources (e.g., print and nonprint texts, artifacts, people) to communicate their discoveries in ways that suit their purpose and audience.

groups of programs: streets and highways, parks and recreation, the military, environmental protection, welfare programs, education, police and fire protection, prisons, regulation of business practices and travel, and much more. A few items were cut from the list as being more in the province of local than national government.

Brian, as the majority leader, brought the joint session of congress to order and told them that for the country to avoid collapse, they had to immediately slash the budget by cutting at least one whole program. Brian asked each subcommittee to rank the importance of the programs they had listed and to write a short proposal for cutting the program they considered least important to the country.

After the groups had finished their rankings and proposals, they were heard on the floor. A debate ensued and a decision was made. In three of the classes it was decided to cut all welfare programs, and in the other two classes all funds to prisons were stopped. "Those people will just have to start paying their own way," said Jack to explain his vote to stop prison funding. "And if they can't, well, too bad. They can boil in their own slime."

For homework, the student senators wrote a diary entry outlining the day's events and their feelings about them. Despite the students' beliefs that they were neither racist nor prejudiced, many students made dismissive and stereotypical comments about the groups who would be affected by the budget cut. It was Judy's hope that the drama work would not only introduce them to the theme of social issues and civil rights, but would position students to evaluate the morality of their thoughts and actions. Brian and Judy believed that the drama could help the students to create new ethical understandings about their place in the world and their ability to act in it. This would be a good stage from which to launch their final projects on social issues and service.

Students develop an understanding of and respect for diversity in language use, patterns, and dialects across cultures, ethnic groups, geographic regions, and social roles.

Students participate as knowledgeable, reflective, creative, and critical members of a variety of literacy communities.

On the next day, as congress reconvened to discuss how to raise money to solve existing problems, a message was brought that aliens from outer space had come to make an offer. Judy, as the alien spokesperson, entered dressed in a robe and hat. She had found that one or two props sometimes helped to jump-start a difficult part of the drama.

There was silence in the senate chambers. Judy announced the space traders' desire to offer America everything needed to repair its economy and environment. The senate would have three days to accept or reject the offer. If they did not accept, there were other countries who would. Judy stepped aside to allow the students to consider the proposal and ask questions.

In every class, someone eventually asked: "What do you want in return?" And the reply: "Your least valued members of society, by your own admission. We will take everyone on welfare with us (or all prisoners) and leave you with all you need for a prosperous tomorrow."

Some senators wanted to know what would be done with the people the space traders wanted. Would they be treated well? What would happen to them?

"That is none of your concern," Judy responded coolly. "We are making a trade. If you do not want what we offer, we will go elsewhere."

She departed and a preliminary vote was taken. In each class, the senators voted to accept the deal. They then voted with their feet by situating themselves along a personal continuum of how strongly they agreed or disagreed with the decision.

The senators were interviewed by Brian, as a radio host, on their vote and opinions. The continuum line was then folded, with students on opposing sides walking over to converse with each other. Students were then allowed to change their positions and were interviewed about their change.

Each night, during the drama, students recorded the events of the day and their evaluation of them in their role as a character. Brian and Judy believed that students needed to do more than experience the perspectives of others or reflect generally on the day's activities. They needed to evaluate the day's decisions and actions. That night, Melissa wrote, that "I'm not going to make any quick judgments about this 'being.' I don't want to make any foolish mistakes on the future of this nation. This 'being' could be lying to us."

Students apply a wide range of strategies to comprehend, interpret, evaluate, and appreciate texts. They draw on their prior experience, their interactions with other readers and writers, their knowledge of word meaning and other texts, their word identification strategies, and their understanding of textual features (e.g., sound-letter correspondence, sentence structure, context, graphics).

On the third day of the drama, the students became the welfare recipients or prisoners who were being traded to the aliens. First, they went through a *step-by-step drama* in which they imagined how they had come to be on welfare or in prison. Brian asked them to close their eyes and "to imagine that you cannot pay all your bills. Why is this so? What has happened to cause this? When you have imagined this, take a small step backwards." When students had been taken through several steps of their imaginative journey to welfare or prison, they gathered in a circle and shared their stories. They discussed whether it was fair that they be asked to go with the space traders. There was usually a wide range of opinion, sometimes depending on the stories the students had imagined in role.

In role, the students wrote a last letter to their friends or family, because after their departure no further communication would ever be possible. The volunteers were accepted for the first shipment, which would go out tomorrow. That night, Jenny, who had agreed to go on this first shipment, wrote that "I went with the aliens because being in jail was the worst. I'm not so sure I'm going to go with the aliens [now] because some of the others made me think how much I'm going to miss my family and I'll never see them again. So I'm very confused right now."

On the fourth day of the drama, the students were told that in just a few minutes they would be loaded into the cargo bay of the spaceship. They exchanged their feelings and discussed any recourse they might have. Then they imagined themselves on the aliens' planet. They imagined best and worst possible scenarios and created tableaux and captions for these situations. In both cases, each student stepped out of the tableau to explain how she felt about being in that situation.

Several short vignettes were played between the aliens and the humans before students were returned to their original roles as senators for the last day of the drama. A renewed debate ensued, a new vote, and students returned themselves to the continuum. Though there was still a variety of opinions, now most students situated themselves towards disagreeing with the trade.

Joe was a student who had expressed near total agreement with the trade on the first day. He wrote about the people on welfare that "it doesn't matter if they die, they're worthless anyway." By Friday, he had moved to total disagreement with the trade. He told Brian, "I've changed my mind. You can't decide for people. Even if we need the money, we can't make them go—they're people too." Joe had evaluated his own actions, connected words with deeds, and changed his ethical stance towards the trade.

Students apply a wide range of strategies to comprehend, interpret, evaluate, and appreciate texts. They draw on their prior experience, their interactions with other readers and writers, their knowledge of word meaning and other texts, their word identification strategies, and their understanding of textual features (e.g., sound-letter correspondence, sentence structure, context, graphics).

Students conduct research on issues and interests by generating ideas and questions, and by posing problems. They gather, evaluate, and synthesize data from a variety of sources (e.g., print and nonprint texts, artifacts, people) to communicate their discoveries in ways that suit their purpose and audience.

Tammy had placed herself on the middle of the first continuum and had responded with a "no comment" during the first radio show. After imagining why she, in role, might have needed public assistance, she wrote, "I don't think we should force them to go. That would be very inhuman. We should give them a choice if they want to go or not." She added that "we probably don't really understand their situation."

Students were asked to revisit their first diary entries and to evaluate if, how, and why their positions and feelings had changed during the drama.

Students conduct research on issues and interests by generating ideas and questions, and by posing problems. They gather, evaluate, and synthesize data from a variety of sources (e.g., print and nonprint texts, artifacts, people) to communicate their discoveries in ways that suit their purpose and audience.

After leaving the drama, the students brainstormed social issues faced by today's society. They came up with quite a list: racism, sexism, ageism, student rights, environmental issues, equal opportunity, helping the poor, handicapped rights, crime and violence, illiteracy, and more. Judy asked the students to write about why one of these issues was of importance and what things had been done or could be done to address it.

The team—including Brian, Judy, Peter, and Matt—took the opportunity to identify over one hundred people, groups, events, and decisions that illustrated the history of the student-identified social issues and efforts to address them. They created note cards entitled with the topics and asked the students to find enough information to fill out the card they had selected so that other members of the class would understand the five W's and H (who, what, where, when, why, and how). Over the next two days, students completed the note cards and a picture to go with them and used them to create a *timeline* of significant ideas and events regarding social issues in our country. The timeline was hung in Judy's classroom to serve as a context and springboard for their project on social issues and social change. In groups, students read through the timeline cards and completed a chart that classified different social problems and what attempts had been made to rectify them.

Students adjust their use of spoken, written, and visual language (e.g., conventions, style, vocabulary) to communicate effectively with a variety of audiences and for different purposes.

Students conduct research on issues and interests by generating ideas and questions, and by posing problems. They gather, evaluate, and synthesize data from a variety of sources (e.g., print and nonprint texts, artifacts, people) to communicate their discoveries in ways that suit their purpose and audience.

Students participate as knowledgeable, reflective, creative, and critical members of a variety of literacy communities.

The students were then invited to begin thinking about a research or service project about a social issue to pursue for their final project. If students chose a service project, they would actually *do* something in the school or community to try and address a social issue. Their research would entail studying the issue and their own success in addressing it. Students could form their own groups and would have two weeks to come up with a written proposal, including a question or problem to address and a plan for doing so. There would be another two weeks to find and read information and to revise topics and research questions before the project hit full stride.

In the meantime, students would spend class time in a shared reading of Mildred Taylor's *Roll of Thunder, Hear My Cry!* Homework time would be spent reading some stories, poems, and articles about various social issues, provided by Judy, and pursuing their own initial background research for their proposed project.

Judy agreed with Nel Noddings (1984, 51) that caring is and must be our "basic reality." She wanted her work with literacy to connect students to the world and to taking on the responsibility to extend the circle of care she hoped had been formed in the classroom. Through the drama, and now through their reading and projects, she asked students to be open to difference, aware of prejudice, tolerant of diverse views and ways of being in the world. She wanted them to become critical of stereotypes and to search for deeper understandings. Education was not just about cognition and knowledge; it was about ethics and affect and understanding. She urged her students to listen to new voices, to question assumptions, and, most of all, to care. This was what moving out into the world was all about. She knew that it was a rocky and perilous journey, but she hoped that her classroom would help to further them on a path towards ethical understanding and action in the world.

Rolling Thunder

Judy knew from experience that students loved to read *Roll of Thunder, Hear My Cry!* Was it the injustice it described? The protagonists of a similar age? The surprises and dilemmas? The love and courage the family expressed in the face of Mississippi racism in the depths of the Great Depression? How the family worked for justice? Judy didn't know, but she was glad for the power the story exerted over her students. There were a few books, she knew, would engage all of her students in an intense transaction, and these were the ones she liked to use for shared readings. At other times, it was more appropriate and fruitful for students to be pursuing and sharing their own reading agendas, and both classtime (most Fridays) and especially homework time provided for that.

While her class read this young adult novel, Peter had students reading primary documents regarding citizenship and social issues: historical pieces, poems, protest speeches, songs. Though they were now sharing and discussing readings in his class, the project groups would pursue their own material as the time for the project neared. Peter felt confident that by now students knew how and would be organized enough to find most of their own information. And they knew what to do and who to ask if they were "jammed," as the students liked to say.

Students read a wide range of print and nonprint texts to build an understanding of texts, of themselves, and of the cultures of the United States and the world; to acquire new information; to respond to the needs and demands of society and the workplace; and for personal fulfillment. Among these texts are fiction and nonfiction, classic and contemporary works.

Judy began by reading the first few chapters of *Roll of Thunder* aloud. She liked what Aidan Chambers wrote, that giving students reading to do is an assignment, but "reading to them is a gift." She knew that once the story had hooked them, the book would move from "gotta read" status to "wanna read" status.

Judy knew that hearing texts read aloud, including the students' own work, was to participate in a linguistic enactment. The teacher, as expert reader, could model how to orally interpret text and monitor meanings and could serve as a mediator facilitating the student-text transaction by modeling what one good reader did and thought while reading. Hearing texts also gave students access to more sophisticated and complex texts than they could read on their own. The teacher, as performer of the text, could embody subtle shades of meaning and support and guide students by stopping to scaffold student response through interaction—doing think-alouds, asking questions, comparing experiences (Cochran-Smith, 1988).

Students apply a wide range of strategies to comprehend, interpret, evaluate, and appreciate texts. They draw on their prior experience, their interactions with other readers and writers, their knowledge of word meaning and other texts, their word identification strategies, and their understanding of textual features (e.g., sound-letter correspondence, sentence structure, context, graphics).

Each evening for homework the students were asked to keep a diary as one of the characters and to ask a few "Tell Me . . ." or QAR questions they wished to pursue through classroom discussion the next day. Discussions took place for a few minutes in small groups, which would usually report to the large group.

On a couple of occasions, Judy set up coffee-can discussions, with students throwing a written question or concern regarding the reading into a coffee can. Groups picked out two or three sheets of paper from the can and used the questions written there to start their discussions.

All of the discussions were led by the students, who by now were monitoring and posing both reading problems and story problems to themselves and to each other. Judy occasionally jumped into the discussions to add information or point out items of significance. Approximately 10 minutes into the period, the class would begin reading again. After the first few chapters, students had the choice of reading with Judy or peeling off into reciprocal reading groups. By Chapter 8, all of the students were in groups, but they reconvened as a class to read the last two chapters aloud.

The diaries were pursued throughout the reading of *Role of Thunder.* After the episode with the bus and the night riders, the students composed four entries, speaking with the voice of Stacey, the oldest boy in the Logan family: (1) when he had formulated the plan to disable the bus full of white children that splashed and ran the family off the road each day; (2) after the plan had been successful; (3) when he thought the night riders were coming to burn out his family's home because of what he had done; and (4) when he found out the truth and knew that his family was safe. In class, the students then conducted role interviews with Stacey about this chain of events.

After Cassie had taken her revenge on Lillian Jean Simms for her racist comments and actions, students composed three entries as Cassie: (1) after Mr. Simms had humiliated her and pushed her off the sidewalk; (2) as she made her plans after promising Papa that no one would ever learn of her revenge against Lillian Jean; and (3) after the revenge was complete.

Students also kept a running chart of significant events surrounding racism in the book: each act of injustice, the perpetrator, the victim, the act of resistance or revenge, the consequences of the resistance, and the reader's commentary, including personal comparisons and evaluation of what had transpired. At the end of the book, students used this chart to analyze patterns. They then wrote about the author's implicit message concerning what kinds of attitudes and actions could help to fight and overcome racism and which actions could not. Again, the focus was on social issues and the theme of social change.

On a couple of occasions as they read, and usually in response to a student question, the students created scenes that were highly significant but missing from the book. For example, they brainstormed what might have happened and been said in the car between Uncle Hammer and Mr. Morrison, then wrote and role played the scene. Students playing the roles of Jeremy and Stacey, Lillian Jean and Cassie, Uncle Hammer and Papa, Big Ma and Mr. Jamison exchanged letters and created choral montages.

At the end of the book, the students requested to create SSRs of their favorite scene. Judy agreed and asked them to layer in a cutout of the author and to comment on who they thought the author was, why she wrote the way she did, and when they might have been aware of her presence in the story. She also asked the students to consider the tone of the scene they were performing and, if they could, to add a creative element such as a background or music that would help the audience to appreciate the mood of the scene. About fifteen students used music during this performance, and one student composed his own music to accompany the SSR.

At the end of their reading, the class played a game Judy called the QAR game. In this game, students wrote significant questions about the book for each other on index cards. For example, "At the end of the book, how was the fire started?" and "What did Mr. Morrison say to Uncle Hammer that night in the car?" ("Think and Search" questions). Judy collected the cards as the students formed into five groups of five or so students. She would recite a question twice and then call on a member of group 1 to identify what kind of question it was. Group 5 acted as judges and awarded or withheld a point. If the answer was incorrect, then anyone from group 2, 3, or 4 could give it a try. If the answer was correct, then the other groups could still get a point if they could show that the readers might make it a different kind of question through what they did to answer it. This was to emphasize to the students that it was the readers' activity to answer a question that made the question a particular type.

Next, the groups would be given a chance to consult together, and one member would be called on to provide as many acceptable answers to the question as possible. This encouraged students to pool their resources and listen to one another, because they never knew who would be called upon to answer.

In the case of "Think and Search" or "Author and Me" questions, there were many possible valid answers. It didn't take the class long to figure out that nearly any answer to an "On Your Own" question would earn a point. The groups then rotated, with group 2 being on the spot, group 1 serving as judges, and the other groups serving as vultures ready to plunge in and get their share of the plunder.

The game was lively and served to review important events and issues from the story and to reinforce the richness and diversity of individual readings. At the end of the game, Judy pulled out her omnipresent bag of treats, stickers, and health food snacks to reward the deserving. She stocked the bag throughout the year, and it was well worth the money she spent.

From a menu of options, most students chose to create a video news show as their final project for the book. Judy provided these groups with information about T. J.'s trial from *Let the Circle Be Unbroken* (the sequel to *Roll of Thunder*), devised criteria for the show with the students, and set them off. They had a day to write scripts, a day to revise and rehearse, and a day to film and free read, and a final day to watch and evaluate the completed videos.

Roll of Thunder, Hear My Cry!
News Show
Criteria Sheet

Theme of the Show: The Struggle for Equality!
News Time: The Day after TJ's Trial
Content:
Each person in your group needs to write one script that will cover some important events and ideas from the book.

Top News Story: TJ's trial
This script is required. Your script, including any re-enactments, exhibits, music, maps and props you might choose to use, should cover the Who, What, Why, Where, When and How of TJ's trial and the importance of the trial's outcome

The remaining scripts for the show should feature, when taken together, at least 10 important events or ideas from the book, Roll of Thunder, Hear My Cry! Again, each event should feature the 5 W's and H and its significance. Each script will include several important ideas. For example, a weather report might include the rains in October and November, and the thunderstorm and fire at the end of the book.

Format:
The newscast should be performed as a news show, including five of the following formats.

Top news story - T.J.'s trial
Feature
Interview
Ad/public service announcement
Sports and/or Weather
Commentary (editorial) - this could be about T.J.'s trial
MTV video spot

Each script will be graded on the criteria of
correctness
thoroughness
thoughtfulness
creativity

Script sign-ups due tomorrow.
Go for it! Scripts due on Wednesday!

T.J's Trial

- All rise for Judge Danielson
judge - Order, I say order in the court.
Today we have the trial of T.J. Avery.
We hear that the death of Mr. Barnett
wz caused by this young man. Today
we will find out the truth.
Mr. Jamison please call your first
witness to the stand.
Mr. Jamison - Thank you your honor. My
first witness is Mrs. Barnett.
(look at sheet with statement)
Mr. Jamison 2nd last - (read relation to mrs. Barnett's statement)
Mrs. Barnett first - (read statement on white sheet)
→ Mrs Barnett please tell the jury & everyone else
what had happened the night 3 men
entered your store & Killed your husband
Mr. Jim Lee Barnett.
→ mrs. Barnett read statement

Mr. Jamison - No further questions - Thank you
Mrs. Barnett

judge - Mr. Jamison your next witness will
approach the stand after this recess. (Go To Sports)

The Final Projects

By now, the students had chosen their groups and made their final project applications. Peter, Judy, and Matt were ready to combine classes again for the last weeks of the year. They were sailing into the unknown, as they had never allowed their students so much freedom to go in their own directions before.

Students conduct research on issues and interests by generating ideas and questions, and by posing problems. They gather, evaluate, and synthesize data from a variety of sources (e.g., print and nonprint texts, artifacts, people) to communicate their discoveries in ways that suit their purpose and audience.

Students develop an understanding of and respect for diversity in language use, patterns, and dialects across cultures, ethnic groups, geographic regions, and social roles.

About 70 of the 130 students had chosen to create a video documentary on a topic of civil rights or social change. One group was researching the Holocaust with the question "What was it like to be in a concentration camp?" Two groups were researching breaking the color barrier in baseball, and another group, including Troy, was reporting on the life of Hank Aaron and the question "What made Hank so great?" Some groups, like Stephanie and Diana's group, were doing the history of the Underground Railroad; and others were focusing on Harriet Tubman, the history of the women's rights movement, the current status of women in the world today, the Vietnam war protest movements, gun control, life during the Depression, and more.

Some groups had taken up the challenge of pursuing a service project. One group was going to help the senior citizens' home near school to plant gardens and would create a video reporting on the experience. Another group was doing a gender equity awareness project; another was organizing a project to clean the lakeshore and riverfront in town; one group was going to work to support a medical mission in East Africa.

Still another group was creating a museum exhibit about student rights and responsibilities, and another—including Kae—was creating a picture book series about child slavery and labor. Kae, who had come to the United States, via Laos and Thailand, had some personal stories she wished to tell on this count.

Rod and Tim, both LD and self-proclaimed hypermedia animation experts, proposed to create a series of animated political cartoons on the topic of animal rights. One they had story-boarded was about a cow in a business suit who had been invited to a company barbecque. Mike wanted to work alone to create a hypercard stack on the pros and cons of dropping the atom bomb. His grandfather had fought in the Pacific campaign, and this issue had been in the news. So Mike was quite excited and enthusiastic about the project.

It was exciting and scary. The team had worked hard over the past weeks to help each group come up with a good topic, question, and action plan that they were eager to tackle. But never had Judy had so many different students going in so many directions, both physically and intellectually. "I'm getting ready to freak out," she told Peter on the day they got started doing the project full time.

Again, they had general checksheets and asked students for a daily journal and plan, a weekly assessment and conference, and lots of peer exchange. "

On the first day, Peter urged the students "to take control of this project and make it something you're proud of. Ask yourself, 'What can we get out of this? Where does this take us in the world? What does or could this mean for the future and for others in our community?' Let's ask 'What if?' instead of saying 'We should do such and such.' Let's ask 'What do *we* think and what can we learn and what can we do?' instead of just asking 'What do the experts say?' This is real research, and you're going to find out what happens when you take certain actions. Good luck!"

Because the majority of students would be creating video documentaries of

NAME:______________________

VIDEO DOCUMENTARY
INDIVIDUAL CRITERIA CHECKLIST

____ 1. TOPIC SELECTION SHEET WITH RATIONALE

____ 2. DOCUMENTARY RESPONSE SHEET FOR AT LEAST ONE DOCUMENTARY THAT YOU HAVE VIEWED ON YOUR OWN.

____ 3. INDIVIDUAL BIBLIOGRAPHY OF WORKS YOU WILL READ; MUST INCLUDE ONE BOOK, PERIODICAL ARTICLE AND CREATIVE RESOURCE

____ 4. READING AND LEARNING LOGS FOR 400 TOTAL MINUTES OR MORE REGARDING MATERIALS YOU HAVE READ RELATING TO YOUR TOPIC.

____ 5. ORGANIZING QUESTION FOR DOCUMENTARY AND LIST OF SUBTOPICS AND KEY DETAILS TO BE COVERED IN YOUR VIDEO.

____ 6. MATERIALS OR PROPERTIES YOU HAVE CREATED TO BE USED IN THE DOCUMENTARY

____ 7. AN OUTLINE OF A VIDEO SCRIPT YOU HAVE CREATED FOR YOUR GROUP INCLUDING CREATIVE REPRESENTATIVE TECHNIQUES SUCH AS ART, VISUALS, INTERVIEWS, MUSIC, COMMENTARY, RE-ENACTMENTS, ETC.

____ 8. A FINAL SCRIPT FOR A SCENE YOU HAVE CREATED

____ 9. EVIDENCE THAT A PEER HAS REVIEWED AND GIVEN FEEDBACK ON YOUR SCRIPT.

____ 10. EVIDENCE OF SCRIPT REVISION: ADDITIONS, CLARIFICATIONS

____ 11. REFLECTIVE PERSONAL JOURNAL REGARDING WHAT AND HOW YOU LEARNED DURING THE DOCUMENTARY PROJECT.

a research question or about their service project, the class began by viewing a short professional documentary about the civil rights movement. They then wrote a review that identified some of the ways that information was represented for the audience: photos with narration, music, maps, reenactments, video footage, interviews.

They then watched three student video documentaries, ranked and evaluated them. As they created a rubric for a student documentary, they discussed how the rubric was adequate or needed adaptations to serve for other kinds of projects like museum exhibits or picture books. Each group then undertook to compose a group rubric for its particular project. In essence, each group was creating its own critical standards.

Despite the fiery pep talk, the students' prior experiences as designers, and a raft of good intentions, there were problems. The course of true learning never did run smooth, Judy guessed. The team received anonymous hate mail from someone who informed them that it was not their job to "further liberal agendas with our children," but "to deliver the facts and content knowledge decided upon by the board of education."

On the one hand, they wanted to dismiss the letter because of its anonymity, but on the other hand they wanted to ask themselves some hard questions. *Were* they furthering a liberal agenda or were they, as they intended, really just helping students to take control over their own education? It was worth some wide-awake discussion and thought. And, too, a theme of their teaching the past few years had been conversation. The team felt that everything started with standards: it was a necessity to ask what they wanted children to know and do, and to ask how as teachers they might best serve those ends. Then it was necessary to converse with others about their methods and to justify and adapt what they were doing, on the basis of those conversations.

Judy liked to quote from Milton's *Areopagitica:* "Truth was never bested by a bad argument." "If we're wrong, we sure as heck want to find out and be helped," she told Peter, "and if we're on the right track, we want to help others and be helped to further ourselves along that path. What's the downside of being aware of what you do and conversing about it? I can't see one! This job is too important to do alone and without scrutiny."

A week into the project, there was a gang break-in at the school. One group wanted to change their topic completely and study the effect of gangs on the school. After two meetings and a new proposal to pursue the questions Why do kids join gangs and how does it affect them if they do? the team approved the switch. Other groups were also revising their topics and questions. By now this kind of revision was regarded as a natural part of the learning process, instead of an added problem or extra work.

Then the team had to deal with the physical problem of keeping track of students. There were the research stations in the classroom and library, as well as two video stations in small conference rooms, and some students needed to use computers or to go out into the community to visit, for example, the senior citizen center. The team arranged the necessary permissions and chaperones, but sometimes a group would end up videotaping without constant supervision. So they had discussions about that and whether kids could be trusted with the video equipment. "Who is the equipment for, anyway?" was what Judy asked herself, as she explained that the team was very careful about leaving kids on their own. But how could they become independent learners unless they were

Students apply a wide range of strategies to comprehend, interpret, evaluate, and appreciate texts. They draw on their prior experience, their interactions with other readers and writers, their knowledge of word meaning and other texts, their word identification strategies, and their understanding of textual features (e.g., sound-letter correspondence, sentence structure, context, graphics).

Students participate as knowledgeable, reflective, creative, and critical members of a variety of literacy communities.

Students use spoken, written, and visual language to accomplish their own purposes (e.g., for learning, enjoyment, persuasion, and the exchange of information).

given the chance to be independent? How could they learn to be trustworthy if they weren't trusted? How could they succeed if they did not have the opportunity to fall short of a worthy challenge? This was what Judy thought was wrong with teacher-proof, child-proof, and fail-proof curriculum: you might play it safe, but nothing was learned; no adventure was experienced.

Judy felt very much like a facilitator, enabler, and justifier on behalf of the kids and their requests. It was a far cry from how she had typically taught. She often heard herself saying, "I'll get back to you on that." "I'll try and arrange that for you." "That sounds like a good idea, what can I do to help you?" She carried around a legal pad with notes about arrangements or materials to get for the students to help them pursue and create their way through the project.

When conferencing with the groups, the team found that they were revisiting a lot of the central themes and "big" learning processes they had worked on all year. Questioning, finding information, organizing, and representing data—all of these skills were being used again, and ever more independently. For example, many students were critiquing and revising their questions without outside help.

The curriculum had become recursive and circular instead of linear. Judy found that she had become more of a problem poser for the groups, continually upping the ante, asking questions, and posing challenges that were tougher and more thought-provoking. She was able to individualize instruction in a way she hadn't before, meeting each kid where she was currently situated and asking for a little harder consideration of the issues.

On the checklists, the team asked for a clear organizing research question.

Students conduct research on issues and interests by generating ideas and questions, and by posing problems. They gather, evaluate, and synthesize data from a variety of sources (e.g., print and nonprint texts, artifacts, people) to communicate their discoveries in ways that suit their purpose and audience.

Students participate as knowledgeable, reflective, creative, and critical members of a variety of literacy communities.

The service learning groups asked open-ended action research questions, such as "What good things will happen if we help the senior citizens plant a garden?" or "What benefits will there be to cleaning up the lakeshore?" These groups interviewed senior citizens, a representative of the natural resources department, and others as they pursued their answers. They observed and kept journals about their work. They read and consulted with others. They were engaging in a primary, hands-on kind of research.

So as the groups gathered information, they began organizing it for their video documentary, exhibit, or final report. The team was pleased that the groups spontaneously used issue trees and webs before writing scripts or sections for their presentation. Again, instead of teaching new techniques, the team found themselves asking questions to extend student understanding or tool use and to problematize issues. "What else might you consider?" "Why do you think that is the best way to present the material?" "Does your issue tree provide enough specific details to convince your audience?" "What have you done to find out about the perspective of X?"

Drama as Research

As the groups created first drafts of their documentaries and reports, many were quite critical of the results. The team, in their role of problem posers, also worked hard to push the students.

Troy was displeased with his own script about Hank Aaron's time in the Negro and minor leagues and with his group's complete show. "It's boring," he complained, "people are going to fall asleep watching it."

"Was your question interesting enough?" Judy asked, "or did you miss something that could have been exciting?"

Their question's current status was "What did Hank Aaron do to become great?" Basically, their answer was that he had practiced a lot and worked hard to make his way to the top. "Practice and work," Judy mused. "Was that all there was to it? Was there anything else that would make his story different from that of other ballplayers?"

"He's different because he was the greatest hitter ever," Andy offered.

"Other ballplayers work hard. What was different about his story?"

Steven was reading Hank's autobiography, *Oh, Henry!* and he offered that "things were different because he was black and people didn't like that he was breaking white people's records." Steven then reported to the group about the hate mail Hank received while nearing Babe Ruth's home run record, and Troy joined in with Hank's struggles with prejudice in the minor leagues.

"Do all great ballplayers go through this," Judy asked, "or is this a unique part of his story that needs to be told to answer your question?"

The group decided that they needed to include the personal struggles and tribulations of Hank in their video to show that much of what he did to achieve greatness occurred off of the ballfield. But the group struggled with how to understand and portray his perspective.

Then Troy had a brainstorm: "Let's use drama!" he exulted. Troy realized that drama was a way to both understand other perspectives and to portray them. Drama had become a method in Troy's learning repertoire. Judy thought the idea was great and agreed to try and help them set up some drama work, but Andy suggested, "Let's call Dr. Edmiston and see if he'll help us?" The call went out to this invaluable community resource, and Dr. E agreed to come in and help the group.

Word spread fast, and soon seven other groups asked to work with Dr. Edmiston to use drama as a research technique. Each group signed up to work with him for two class sessions over the course of the next week. Two other groups couldn't match schedules, and Judy agreed to work with these groups after school.

The sessions started off with the groups reporting on their question, findings, problems, and dissatisfactions. They brought in their current data, photographs, and other artifacts that could be used to inform the drama work.

The group working on Vietnam war protests didn't understand why the protests were necessary, because "How could anybody support the war?" Brian asked them if they remembered Desert Storm, and they discussed the reasons for that war and the arguments against it. They began their drama by protesting at a military recruitment center. They then interviewed the recruiter on his views.

The next drama was played out as a family with one son in the military, and one who was just returning from Woodstock. The family received word that their first son was missing in action, and they played out the scene. The students later took on the roles of soldiers in the field, of Vietnamese peasants, and of Pentagon officials deciding whether to escalate the war effort. They then returned to their original role of protesters meeting to outline an effective plan of protest that would serve to change people's minds about the war.

The group asked a whole series of questions as they pursued their drama research. They started by asking about how people protested the war, then asked about the effects of various protests. Then they asked why people felt so strongly about the war, on both sides of the issue, and how the protests affected

Students apply a wide range of strategies to comprehend, interpret, evaluate, and appreciate texts. They draw on their prior experience, their interactions with other readers and writers, their knowledge of word meaning and other texts, their word identification strategies, and their understanding of textual features (e.g., sound-letter correspondence, sentence structure, context, graphics).

Students adjust their use of spoken, written, and visual language (e.g., conventions, style, vocabulary) to communicate effectively with a variety of audiences and for different purposes.

Students conduct research on issues and interests by generating ideas and questions, and by posing problems. They gather, evaluate, and synthesize data from a variety of sources (e.g., print and nonprint texts, artifacts, people) to communicate their discoveries in ways that suit their purpose and audience.

people who were in the military or who had family members in the service. What was the purpose of the war? How did it affect the Vietnamese people? They eventually ended with the question: How did popular music work as a way of protesting the war?

Two girls in the Depression group couldn't understand why people couldn't get jobs, and their group of four participated in dramas that helped them to experience joblessness, job competition, a move across the country, and life in a Hooverville. This was a form of phenomenological research in which the students tried to enter into the individual experience of people in the social situation that they were researching.

Celia, who had refused to believe that no work was available for people who wanted it, wrote that "The drama kind of helped me to see that it *was* hard to find work and that it would be really frustrating if you couldn't help yourself. You had to do more for yourself than we do now. I admire my grandparents now for living through it."

The group compared possible solutions to the problems of the Depression with those offered by President Roosevelt in his New Deal.

All of the groups constantly interrogated their drama work for accuracy. "According to what we know, did this kind of thing happen? Might it have happened? If it happened, what might its effect have been?"

Students develop an understanding of and respect for diversity in language use, patterns, and dialects across cultures, ethnic groups, geographic regions, and social roles.

The group studying Hank Aaron, directed by information that Steven provided, role played significant events through the chronology of Aaron's life. They began in his childhood and then dramatized scenes from the Negro leagues. When he was invited to play in the minors, his teammates tried to prepare him for how life would be different as a minority in Eau Claire, Wisconsin. After role playing some of his struggles in the minors, Hank had to decide whether to continue to pursue his goal to play in the major leagues. At one point, Troy, playing the role of Hank, decided it was too much and that he was going to quit. Brian, in the role of sportscaster, asked Troy how he wanted to be remembered, what legacy he wished to bequeath to the youth of America. By the end of the interview, Troy had decided to continue his quest.

Students apply a wide range of strategies to comprehend, interpret, evaluate, and appreciate texts. They draw on their prior experience, their interactions with other readers and writers, their knowledge of word meaning and other texts, their word identification strategies, and their understanding of textual features (e.g., sound-letter correspondence, sentence structure, context, graphics).

A highpoint of the drama came when Hank was approaching the home run record. His family received a death threat–taken directly from the book–and they had to decide together whether Hank should play that day.

Through the dramas, the students explored the experiences of people affected by the issues they were studying, they considered the culture of times and places removed from them, and they considered action research questions such as "What would have happened if . . . ?" or "What could happen in the future if . . . ?"

Students conduct research on issues and interests by generating ideas and questions, and by posing problems. They gather, evaluate, and synthesize data from a variety of sources (e.g., print and nonprint texts, artifacts, people) to communicate their discoveries in ways that suit their purpose and audience.

The whole project, and the drama work in particular, certainly fit Judy's definition of action research. As described by Kemmis and McTaggart (1988, 7), it is "the way groups of people can organize the conditions under which they can learn from their own experience, and make this experience accessible to others." The students were not only researchers into the content of their chosen social issues, but into their own learning. They were planning, acting, observing, reflecting, and evaluating how their actions as researchers affected their learning. All this to become more thoughtful and reflective in their work.

Students participate as knowledgeable, reflective, creative, and critical members of a variety of literacy communities.

During and after the drama work, the students hurriedly set about reorganizing and rescripting their documentaries. Many of the scenes enacted with Dr. Edmiston were adapted for inclusion in their shows.

Some interesting developments were also occurring through the work of those engaged in service projects. The group at the senior citizen center became interested in many of the stories that they were told there. Two girls, besides helping to plant the garden, interviewed several of the people there about dating rituals over the course of their lifetimes. They created a wonderful video they called "The Dating Game" by splicing sections of those interviews with their classmate's comments about the current dating scene. This group also tipped off the groups studying women's rights and the one hoping to inform the school about gender equity issues to come over and interview some of the senior women. As a result of the interviews, one group changed the focus of their research to how women's rights and opportunities had changed throughout the century. And several of the women agreed to help the gender equity group with their schoolwide public relations campaign."

Final Sharings

The projects began to take on a life of their own, and the students really rushed to complete their presentations. The major complaint was about the lack of time. That was a good kind of complaint to hear, and showed the students' dedication to and engagement with their projects. The team agreed

Harriet Tubman and the Underground Railroad:
Introduction and Background on the Underground Railroad

She risked her life for more than 300 other people's freedom. She went into areas where she could have easily been killed time and time again because she believed everyone was born equal and should be free. *(picture of an equal sign, maybe have a black person on one side and a white on the other side)* She was strong, physically and mentally. She was often called Moses by people because she led slaves out of the South to freedom in the North like Moses led the Israelites out of Egypt to freedom from the pharaoh and slavery.

Who was this person and how did she save so many people? She was Harriet Tubman and she is often known as the greatest conductor of the Underground Railroad. *(have a picture of Harriet Tubman)*

You may be asking yourself right now: What is the Underground Railroad? *(have person sitting in chair and saying: "Self, what is the Underground Railroad?")*

I'll tell you.

The Underground Railroad was a way for slaves to get to the North and Canada from the South to become free.

It was not really a train *(have a toy train or a picture of a train)* and it was not underground as some people think. Then why in the world *(have a little world)* was it called the Underground Railroad? It was called underground because it was a secret operation and very few people knew about it or saw it while it was going on. It was called a railroad because it was a way to get to the North on certain routes with different places to stop along the way called stations. You can see some of the routes on this map. *(hold up map)*

Stations were the homes of free people who wanted to help the slaves get to freedom. These people who owned the stations were called stationmasters. They were also commonly called abolitionists because they wanted to abolish slavery. they wanted to abolish slavery because they did not think it was right for people to own other people and treat them the way some of the slaves were treated, such as whipping or starving them. *(sign with the word slavery in a circle with a slash through it)*

The stations would often have secret rooms, trap doors or hidden tunnels for the slaves to hide in. Other stations just hid the fugitives in their barn, attics, or potato cellars. There were also hidden compartments or false floors in wagons so they could get the slaves to the next station faster and without being seen. *(picture of hidden compartment in wagon)*

The station masters would supply food and blankets for the runaway slaves while they were at that station.

You could identify which houses were stations by a wide variety of signals. There could be a barn lantern with a special colored shade, a row of bricks painted white on a chimney, or a flag standing in a certain place. *(have picture or 3-D versions of each of these examples to show)* The signs or signals had to visible at night so fugitives could see it since they only traveled when it was dark out.

When the slaves identified a station they would often knock on the door. When asked who they were, they would reply : "A friend with friends" *(have two people acting out this scene)* Another way to show when a runaway had come was to put a dead branch in a pine tree at a certain angle.

It was said earlier that Harriet Tubman was a conductor of the Underground Railroad. So what were the conductors and what did they do? The conductors were probably the bravest and most daring people who helped out with the underground Railroad. These people when down into the South time after time and helped lead the slaves to freedom by showing them to the next station by the fastest and safest routes. They also helped to keep the fugitives spirits up. Harriet Tubman probably saved the most people any conductor ever saved. *(be showing picture of Harriet during last sentence)*

HARRIET TUBMAN AND THE UNDERGROUND RAILROAD

Directions: Put a check by the following statements if you agree with them

____1. Harriet Tubman was a saint who served her country well.

____2. Harriet's bravery and determination to run away and free other slaves proved that she believed in what she was doing.

____3. In her time she was considered a criminal who would have been hung if she was caught.

____4. If Harriet Tubman didn't escape when she did, she would have been a slave forever.

____5. The Underground Railroad was too risky for weak and unsure slaves.

____6. Without Quakers, the Underground Railroad wouldn't have been successful.

____7. Harriet Tubman was the reason why many slaves reached freedom.

that a great mark of success was that every group went through the whole process of the project and made a final presentation.

There was a mini-lesson on creating a prepresentation learning guide and evaluation tool for the project's audience. The audience would read the guide before viewing (to focus their attention on particular issues) and then respond to it after viewing. Each group created one of these to help their audience get the most from their presentation and to help the group evaluate the effectiveness of their presentation as a teaching tool. They also evaluated their own work, that of their group members, and the project as a whole.

After the presentations, the project was concluded by discussing what was still left to be done regarding the issue or service which had been their topic and how the groups or individuals might continue their work in the future.

Because there was no time to do the kind of family portfolio presentations that they had planned, the class tried to work out another way to end the year. They decided to spend the last few days of school preparing their portfolios and to present these in groups during the final exam periods. The students decided that the portfolio would include a final SSR or tableau drama of a favorite reading experience from the year. Judy asked that the portfolios be entitled "Me as a Literacy Learner," and the group discussed what other items could be included. Judy also asked that the students review their projects, letters, and journals to research their own growth as designers over the course of the year. She asked them to include a letter or essay outlining that growth in their portfolio. In this way, the students would be making another pass at researching themselves as learners.

On the final exam day, groups of five students took fifteen minutes each to present their portfolios to the classmates in their group. The students had also invited some guests to attend the presentations. Judy and Matt milled about the classroom trying to catch at least five minutes or so of each presentation and to keep things moving along. The students in the audience composed written evaluations of each presentation, which they passed to the presenter. These evaluations were read and then given to Judy.

As part of the portfolio they submitted, students had requested the grade they wanted and justified it in a cover letter that explained the learning and growth that was demonstrated by the contents of the portfolio. They also evaluated the course and made suggestions of how to improve it during the coming year.

As Judy read through the portfolios and suggestions, she kept a running list of goals for next year. She thought about how to deal with the constraints of time and physical space, of ways to bring even more community members into the school, how to extend the service projects that had really just served as pilots. She thought about how to converse and work with her students' future teachers to share their interests and extend the kind of work they had done this year.

Judy always felt sentimental about saying goodbye to her students, and right now she intensely wished that she could keep working with these kids, because she knew them now and liked them so well. Wouldn't it be great, she asked

Peter, to take a group of sixth graders and work with them through the three years of middle school? Think of what had been done in one year! How much more they could do in three years!

As Judy thought about the school year just past, she once again picked up her copy of the national standards. How had the methods she used with her students helped them to approach what they needed to know and be able to do? Were there important issues she had slighted, like investigating and considering language in use and language diversity? How could she do better? Would she amend some standards as she used them as a compass for her future teaching journeys? How might the standards help her in future conversations with her own practice, her students, and colleagues?

She thought of Robert Frost and "how road leads on to road" and how a teaching journey ended is always another teaching journey begun. Standards, whether national, local, or personal, were vitally important, but they would never be more than an astrolabe or a gyroscope for the teaching soul. The journey and its map of stories had to be created by individual teachers and students, through their walking and travelling under the sun and the stars.

As Freire and Horton (1990) had entitled one of Judy's favorite teaching books: "We make the road by walking."

Judy was glad to have walked this road with her students, and she was eager to see what roads they would make and walk together in the future.

Only where love and need are one,
And the work is play for mortal stakes,
Is the deed ever really done
For Heaven and the future's sake.

—Robert Frost, "Two Tramps in Mudtime"

Some Standards Highlighted

Meaning: Students pursue shared and individual readings and a small-group research project to understand the nature of social issues and citizenship and how individual citizens can work for change. Some students provide a service to the community during their final project. Students present their research findings through video documentary and other means.

Fluency and control: Students use a variety of strategies to read, lead their own discussions, do drama and debate, research and create documents of their findings.

Critical analysis: Students develop individual rubrics for their projects. They explore the meaning of literature through a variety of question types and strategies. Students integrate a variety of information from various sources into a coherent whole as they create their final project.

Knowledge acquisition: Students learn about the history of social issues in America and the civil rights movement and study the effect of racism on one family living through the Depression. They use video and other creative representations to demonstrate their understandings.

Creativity: Students use drama as a research technique to pursue understanding of their research question. Students use reenactments, artwork, and a variety of other creative formats to present their findings.

Cultural diversity: Students read and discuss the situation of a minority family in the South during the 1930s through the novel *Roll of Thunder, Hear My Cry!* They attempt to understand the relationship betwen social issues, social justice, and various subgroups in our culture.

Resources

Writing to Learn

Ackerman, J. (1993). The promise of writing to learn. *Written Communication,10* (3), 334–370.

Elbow, P. (1973). *Writing without teachers.* New York: Oxford University Press.

Elbow, P. (1981). *Writing with power: Techniques for mastering the writing process.* New York: Oxford University Press.

Emig, J. (1977). Writing as a mode of learning. *College Composition and Communication, 28* (2), 122–128.

Gere, A. R. (Ed.). (1985). *Roots in the sawdust: Writing to learn across the disciplines.* Urbana, IL: National Council of Teachers of English.

Mayher, J. S., Lester, N. B., & Pradl, G. M. (1983). *Learning to write/writing to learn.* Upper Montclair, NJ: Heinemann, Boynton/Cook.

Moffett, J. (1981). *Active voice: A writing program across the curriculum.* Upper Montclair, NJ: Heinemann, Boynton/Cook.

Murray, D. M. (1984). *Write to learn.* New York: Holt, Rinehart and Winston.

Multiple Intelligences and Learning with Various Media

Christenbury, L. (Ed.). (1995). *Multiple intelligences.* Special theme issue of *English Journal, 84* (8).

Gallas, K. (1994). *The languages of learning: How children talk, write, dance, draw, and sing their understanding of the world.* New York: Teachers College Press.

Gardner, H. (1983). *Frames of mind: The theory of multiple intelligences.* New York: Basic Books.

Gardner, H. (1993). *Multiple intelligences: The theory in practice.* New York: Basic Books.

Rief, L. (1992). *Seeking diversity: Language arts with adolescents.* Upper Montclair, NJ: Heinemann, Boynton/Cook.

Smagorinsky, P. (1991). *Expressions: Multiple intelligences in the English class.* Urbana, IL: National Council of Teachers of English.

Wilhelm, J. (in press). Reading is seeing: Using visual response to improve the literary reading of reluctant readers. *Journal of Reading Behavior.*

Performance-Based Assessment

Anthony, R. J., Johnson, T. D., Michelson, N. S., & Pearce, A. (1991). *Evaluating literacy: A perspective for change.* Portsmouth, NH: Heinemann, Boynton/Cook.

Glazer, S. M., & Brown, C. S. (1993). *Portfolios and beyond: Collaborative assessment in reading and writing.* Norwood, MA: Christopher-Gordon.

Harp, B. (Ed.). (1991). *Assessment and evaluation in whole language programs.* Norwood, MA: Christopher-Gordon.

Jett-Simpson, M., & Leslie, L. (1994). *Ecological assessment: Under construction.* Schofield, WI: Wisconsin State Reading Association.

Perrone, V. (Ed.). (1991). *Expanding student assessment.* Alexandria, VA: Association for Supervision and Curriculum Development.

Affect and Ethical Imagination

Beane, J. A. (1990). *Affect in the curriculum: Toward democracy, dignity and diversity.* New York: Teachers College Press.

Bogdan, D. (1992). *Re-educating the imagination: Toward a poetics, politics, and pedagogy of literary engagement.* Portsmouth, NH: Heinemann, Boynton/Cook.

Bruner, J. (1986). *Actual minds, possible worlds.* Cambridge, MA: Harvard University Press.

Edmiston, B., & Wilhelm, J. (1995). Drama and the ethical imagination. In B. J. Wagner (Ed.), *What we learn from drama.* Portsmouth, NH: Heinemann, Boynton/Cook.

Gilligan, C. (1982). *In a different voice: Psychological theory and women's development.* Cambridge, MA: Harvard University Press.

Johnson, M. (1993). *Moral imagination: Implications of cognitive science for ethics.* Chicago: University of Chicago Press.

Montessori, M. (1972). *Education and peace.* Chicago: Regnery.

Noddings, N. (1984). *Caring, a feminine approach to ethics and moral education.* Berkeley: University of California Press.

Noddings, N. (1992). *The challenge to care in schools: An alternative approach to education.* New York: Teachers College Press.

Rogers, C. (1969). *Freedom to learn: A view of what education might become.* Columbus, OH: Charles E. Merrill.

WORKS CITED

Atwell, N. (1987). *In the middle: Writing, reading and learning with adolescents.* Upper Montclair, NJ: Boynton/Cook.

Berthoff, A. (1981). *The making of meaning.* Upper Montclair, NJ: Boynton/Cook.

Brown, R. (1992). *Schools of thought: How the politics of literacy shape thinking in the classroom.* San Francisco: Jossey-Bass.

Brown, A., & Palinscar, A. (1989). Guided, cooperative learning and individual knowledge acquisition. In L. Resnick (Ed.), *Knowing, learning and instruction: Essays in honor of Robert Glaser.* Hillsdale, NJ: Erlbaum.

Burnsford, S. (1960). *The incredible journey.* New York: Bantam Starfire.

Chambers, A. (1985). *Booktalk.* London: The Bodley Head.

Cochran-Smith, M. (1988). Mediating: An important role for the reading teacher. In C. Hedley & J. Hicks (Eds.), *Reading and the special learner.* Norwood, NJ: Ablex.

Copperman, P. (1986). *Taking books to heart: How to develop a love of reading in your child.* Reading, MA: Addison-Wesley.

Dewey, J. (1910). *How we think.* Boston: Heath.

Enciso, P. (1990). *The nature of engagement in reading: Profiles of three fifth graders' engagement strategies and stances.* Unpublished doctoral dissertation, Ohio State University, Columbus, OH.

Freire, P., & Horton, M. (1990). *We make the road by walking.* B. Bell, J. Gaventa, & J. Peters (Eds.). Philadelphia: Temple University Press.

Iser, W. (1978). *The act of reading.* Baltimore, MD: Johns Hopkins University Press.

Kemmis, S., & McTaggart, R. (1988). *The action research planner.* Geelong, Victoria, Australia: Deakin University Press.

Kirsch, I. S., & Jungeblut, A. (1986). *Literacy: Profiles of America's young adults.* Princeton, NJ: National Assessment of Educational Progress.

Noddings, N. (1984). *Caring: A feminine approach to ethics and moral education.* Berkeley: University of California Press.

Ogle, D. S. (1986). K-W-L group instruction strategy. In A. Palinscar, D. Ogle, & E. Cart (Eds.), *Teaching reading as thinking*. Alexandria, VA: Association for Supervision and Curriculum Development.

Palinscar, A., & Brown, A. (1984). Reciprocal teaching of comprehension-fostering and comprehension-monitoring activities. *Cognition and Instruction, 1*(2), 117–175.

Perkins, D. N. (1986). Knowledge as design. Hillsdale, NJ: Erlbaum.

Rabinowitz, P. (1987). *Before reading: Narrative conventions and the politics of interpretation*. Ithaca, NY: Cornell University Press.

Raphael, T. (1986). Question-answer relationships. *The Reading Teacher, 36* (6), 516–522.

Rosenblatt, L. (1978). *The reader, the text, the poem: The transactional theory of the literary work*. Carbondale: Southern Illinois University Press.

Smith, F. (1986). *Insult to intelligence: The bureaucratic invasion of our classroom*. New York: Arbor House.

Taylor, M. (1976). *Roll of thunder, hear my cry!* New York: Dial.

Author

Jeffrey Wilhelm has been a teacher of reading and the language arts at the middle and secondary school level for the past thirteen years. His interests include team teaching, co-constructing inquiry-driven curriculum with students, and pursuing teacher research. His recent research agenda includes studying how student reading and thinking can be supported through the use of art, drama, and technology. He also enjoys speaking, presenting, and working with schools and students.

He currently is an assistant professor at the University of Maine where he teaches courses in middle- and secondary-level literacy. In Maine, he coordinates the fledgling Adolescent Literacy Project and summer institutes in literacy and technology. He is also the recent recipient of the NCTE Promising Researcher Award (1995) for his dissertation entitled "Developing Readers: Teaching Engaged and Reflective Reading with Young Adolescents."

Other Books from NCTE Related to English Language Arts Content Standards

Standards for the English Language Arts

From the National Council of Teachers of English and the International Reading Association

What should English language arts students know and be able to do? This book—the culmination of more than three years of intense research and discussion among members of the English language arts teaching community, parents, and policymakers—answers this question by presenting standards that encompass the use of print, oral, and visual language and addresses six interrelated English language arts: reading, writing, speaking, listening, viewing, and visually representing. *Standards for the English Language Arts* starts by examining the rationale for standard setting—why NCTE and IRA believe defining standards is important and what we hope to accomplish by doing so. The book then explores the assumptions that underlie the standards, defines and elaborates each standard individually, and provides real-life classroom vignettes in which readers can glimpse standards in practice. Designed to complement state and local standards efforts, this document will help educators prepare all K–12 students for the literacy demands of the twenty-first century. 1996. Grades K–12. ISBN 0-8141-4676-7.

Stock No. 46767-4025
$18.00 nonmembers, $13.00 NCTE members

Standards Consensus Series

Books in this series serve as useful guides for K–12 teachers who are striving to align lively, classroom-tested practices with standards. A survey of local, state, and national documents revealed a broad consensus in the key topics most frequently addressed in standards; clearly local conditions may vary, but English language arts teachers across the country face many common challenges as they help students meet higher literacy standards. These first releases in the Standards Consensus Series draw on these common threads and bring together the best teaching ideas from prior NCTE publications in topical books with practical, everyday applications in the classroom. Among the titles available:

Teaching the Writing Process in High School (ISBN 0-8141-5286-4)
Stock No. 52864-4025
$12.95 nonmembers, $9.95 NCTE members

Teaching Literature in High School: The Novel (ISBN 0-8141-5282-1)
Stock No. 52821-4025
$12.95 nonmembers, $9.95 NCTE members

Teaching Literature in Middle School: Fiction (ISBN 0-8141-5285-6)
Stock No. 52856-4025
$12.95 nonmembers; $9.95 NCTE members

Motivating Writing in Middle School (ISBN 0-8141-5287-2)
Stock No. 52872-4025
$12.95 nonmembers, $9.95 NCTE members

Additional Titles in the Standards in Practice Series

Standards in Practice, Grades K–2 by Linda K. Crafton
(ISBN 0-8141-4691-0)
Stock No. 46910-4025
$15.95 nonmembers, $11.95 NCTE members

Standards in Practice, Grades 3–5 by Martha Sierra-Perry
(ISBN 0-8141-4693-7)
Stock No. 46937-4025
$15.95 nonmembers, $11.95 NCTE members

Standards in Practice, Grades 9–12 by Peter Smagorinsky
(ISBN 0-8141-4695-3)
Stock No. 46953-4025
$15.95 nonmembers, $11.95 NCTE members

Ordering Information

Any of the useful resources described above can be ordered from the National Council of Teachers of English by phoning 1-800-369-6283; by faxing your order to 1-217-328-9645; by e-mailing your order request to <orders@ncte.org>; or by sending your order to NCTE Order Fulfillment, 1111 W. Kenyon Road, Urbana, IL 61801-1096.

To preview these resources, visit the NCTE home page at <http://www.ncte.org>.